W9-AKY-832

barbecue

100 BEST RECIPES

LINDA DOESER

BARNES
&NOBLE
BOOKS
NEW YORK

This edition published by Barnes & Noble Inc.,
by arrangement with Exclusive Editions

2004 Barnes & Noble Books

Copyright © Exclusive Editions 2003

M 10 9 8 7 6 5 4 3 2 1

All rights reserved. No part of this book may be used or reproduced
in any manner whatsoever without written permission of the publisher.

Created and produced by
The Bridgewater Book Company Ltd,
Lewes, East Sussex

Photographer Ian Parsons
Home economists Sara Hesketh & Richard Green

ISBN: 0-7607-5306-7

Printed in China

NOTE

This book uses imperial, metric, or US cup measurements. Follow the same units
of measurement throughout; do not mix imperial and metric. All spoon
measurements are level: teaspoons are assumed to be 5 ml and tablespoons
are assumed to be 15 ml. Unless otherwise stated, milk is assumed to be whole,
eggs and individual vegetables such as potatoes are medium, and pepper
is freshly ground black pepper.

The times given for each recipe are an approximate guide only
because the preparation times may differ according to the techniques used
by different people and the cooking times may vary as a result of the type of
barbecue used, the size and type of grill, the heat level, and the weather
conditions. The preparation times include chilling and
marinating times, where appropriate.

The nutritional information provided for each recipe is per serving
or per portion. Optional ingredients, variations, or serving suggestions
have not been included in the calculations.

Recipes using raw or very lightly cooked eggs should be avoided
by infants, the elderly, pregnant women, convalescents, and anyone
suffering from an illness.

contents

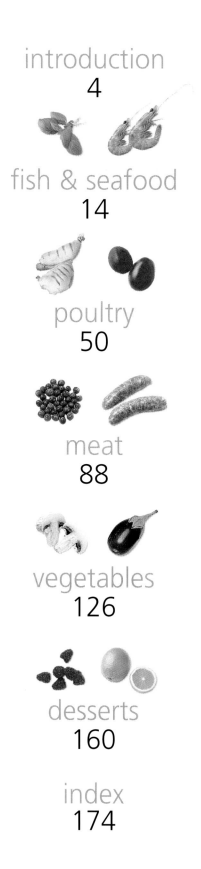

introduction

Barbecues are not only a delicious way of cooking food outside and an interesting alternative to a picnic, they are also healthy and fun. Whether you are cooking a small weekend lunch for the family or throwing a summer party for 20 guests, a barbecue can provide plenty of variety and entertainment for everyone. Let your guests or the family join in and help to cook and serve their own food—even the children can help if they are supervised by an adult.

The idea of a barbecue is very ancient and spans many cultures. Although meat is the traditional staple, vegetarians can also enjoy a wide variety of barbecued dishes. This book features traditional "sausage sizzle" barbecue dishes, as well as more exotic and unusual ones. You can start by cooking simple barbecues, such as sausages, hamburgers, and steaks, until you build up your confidence and become more familiar with your barbecue. When you feel that you are ready to try something more complicated, experiment with meats, vegetables, marinades, and a range of different dishes. You can even practise cooking these dishes under the broiler in your kitchen before serving them from the barbecue at a party. Virtually any type of food can be cooked on a barbecue, from meat, poultry, and seafood to vegetables, tofu, and desserts. You can make kabobs on skewers, use lean cuts of meat with some seasoning, make foil packages, or try out your own ideas. Barbecues are immensely versatile. Try serving a choice of different foods with your main dishes. Baked potatoes and salads are the traditional accompaniments to serve at a barbecue, but you can liven these up. Try putting bowls of different fillings on the table for your guests to have with their baked potatoes—tuna and mayonnaise, creamy cheeses, or a spicy corn relish. It is very easy to add interest to a barbecue. Try a selection of salads—a green salad for traditionalists and a pasta, rice, tomato, or mixed bean salad to add color and extra flavor.

Sweet dishes can also be cooked on the barbecue—simply wrap them in foil packages to keep them away from meat juices. This also works brilliantly if you have vegetarian guests who will not like their vegetables to come into contact with the meat you are cooking.

Try a barbecue birthday party for children, depending on their ages. If you have very young children, it may be safer to keep them away from the barbecue altogether. However, if your children are older, they can help you to choose the menu and prepare and even cook some of the dishes. A barbecue also adds a delightful twist to an ordinary garden party and children will love it.

Most cuisines throughout the world have at least one dish that is wonderful cooked on a barbecue. This book features recipes from across the globe—Caribbean dishes, such as Caribbean Fish Kabobs (see page 16), Jamaican Kabobs (see page 56), and Jerk Chicken (see page 61), and spicy Cajun dishes, such as the traditional Cajun Chicken (see page 52) and the more unusual Cajun Vegetables (see page 147). You can try the Mexican Tuna (see page 30) or Greek Red Snapper Packages (see page 33) if you are a seafood lover. There is spicy Thai Chicken (see page 62) for those who like an Asian flavor to their food and Chicken Tikka (see page 72) for those who prefer an Indian influence. Fruity Duck (see page 82) and Butterflied Squab Chickens (see page 84) are impressive dishes for entertaining guests, while Best-Ever Burgers (see page 90) and an Easy Mixed Grill (see page 122) are simpler ones for when you have less time

or energy. There are dishes to suit every palate—Indonesian Beef Kabobs (see page 100) for a meat-lover willing to experiment and Mushroom Burgers (see page 139) for vegetarians with a hearty appetite.

You can serve a dessert as simple as vanilla ice cream, or a grilled one, such as Barbecued Fruit with Maple Syrup (see page 172) or Banana Sizzles (see page 173), as a perfect finale to any barbecue.

types of barbecue

There are many different types of barbecue available and you are sure to find one to suit your specific needs, depending on size and how often you are likely to use it. If you have only one barbecue every summer, it may be sensible just to buy a disposable grill.

When choosing a barbecue, be sure to look around. as there is a large range and the prices can vary drastically. Bear in mind how many people you are likely to be cooking for and how large your garden is. Will the smoke annoy your neighbors? Should you consider a built-in brick barbecue? How much would you like to spend? What sort of fuel would you prefer to use? Plan the type of barbecue you will need for your lifestyle.

- You can make your own barbecue, whether permanent or temporary. Use the materials round you, on the beach, at a picnic, or in your garden. A pile of stones or bricks with small pieces of wood as fuel works well with a rack placed over the top.
- Disposable barbecues are usually little more than a foil tray with a rack resting near the top and this is adequate for a small picnic or lunch. They are inexpensive and the fuel supplied as part of the pack will last for about 1 hour. They can be used only once.
- Portable barbecues vary in size and price and are a popular choice. They are light and easy to carry and fold away to fit into the trunk of a car. These are ideal for a larger picnic where you will not have to walk too far. They are especially easy to clean.

- Brazier barbecues are another popular choice and are portable to a limited extent. Although you could not transport a brazier barbecue to a picnic, it can easily be moved into a shed for storage or to another part of the garden. Some brazier barbecues have legs while others have wheels, but do make sure that the height is convenient for the person who will be doing most of the cooking, as they can sometimes be a little low. If your garden is windy, a brazier may not be the best choice since these are open barbecues, although many do have a hood to offer some protection. Some have shelves attached to the side, which are useful for storing cooking utensils.
- Hibachi barbecues are small and easy to transport. They originate from Japan, where the name translates as "firebox." They are inexpensive and are now usually made from lightweight materials, although they are traditionally made from cast iron.
- Kettle-grill barbecues are versatile and efficient and you can also use them with the lid on for smoking foods. The large lid offers protection from the wind and can rescue a barbecue party if the weather is unfavorable. Many have a spit attachment. Joints of meat or whole chickens can be cooked on this type of barbecue and they are large enough for most families. Meat cooks evenly and it is easy to control the heat using the air vents. These are the best choice for people who do not want a built-in barbecue.
- Gas and electric barbecues are very efficient and you do not have to wait for the coals to heat up, as it takes only 10 minutes for them to warm up. They are a good choice if you are planning to use your barbecue commercially—they tend to be expensive. They are easy to operate, but do not produce the traditional smoky flavor of grilling over charcoal.
- Permanent barbecues are an excellent choice if you plan to barbecue frequently. They can be built to the right size for your family and do not have to be

expensive. Firstly, go out into your garden and choose the best site for your barbecue. It should be a little distance from the house and from your neighbours, but close to the kitchen if possible. You can build your barbecue with simple materials, such as house bricks, but the bricks inside should be firebricks that can withstand the intense heat. You can put a metal grilling rack at whatever height you want—adjustable if you like—and a metal tray for the fuel. You can also purchase packs containing everything you will need.

types of fuel

There are different types of fuel for different types of barbecue and you should consider which type you would prefer to use before buying your barbecue. If you do not feel happy using charcoal or wood, a gas or electric barbecue may be what you need. Be careful to store your fuel in a dry place, whatever type you use.

- Lumpwood charcoal is easy to ignite, but will burn relatively quickly. It is readily available and inexpensive.
- Charcoal briquettes can take a while to ignite, but they burn for a long time with little smell or smoke. They are ideal for a small garden where the barbecue is near windows and other people's houses.
- Self-igniting charcoal is lumpwood charcoal or briquettes that have been coated with a flammable chemical, which will light very easily. You should wait until the chemical has burned off before adding food to the barbecue, as it may give off an undesirable smell, which can taint the food.
- Hardwoods can be used for barbecues. Woods such as oak and apple are best, as they burn slowly and have a pleasant smell. Softwoods are not appropriate, as they burn too fast and will spark. If you are going to use wood as a fuel, remember that it will need constant attention to maintain an even heat. Be careful to keep wood supplies away from the barbecue as flying sparks could ignite them.

- Wood chips and herbs are designed to be added to the fire, not used as a main fuel. Depending on what you are cooking, sprigs of rosemary, thyme, and sage make particularly attractive additions to a barbecue and will give off a delicious aroma. Sprinkle them over the hot coals or wood underneath the food.

getting going

Lighting a barbecue need not be a worry and an effort. It should take only a few minutes, providing that you prepare well and make sure that you have extra fuel nearby. Always follow the instructions that come with the fuel if you are using self-igniting charcoal. Follow these steps for a successful barbecue.

1   Use foil to line the bottom of your barbecue underneath the fire grate. This will make cleaning easier and will keep the bottom of the barbecue hot.
2   Spread a layer of whichever fuel you are using onto the fire grate. Small pieces at the bottom and medium-size pieces on top of them works best. The layer of charcoal or wood should be 2-inches/5-cm deep and resemble a pyramid in the center of the grate.

3 Using firelighter cubes and liquid is most effective, but you should be able to light your barbecue with just one or the other. If using firelighter cubes, place one or two cubes in the center of the pyramid. If using liquid firelighter, pour a few tablespoons into the fuel and leave for a minute. Light the barbecue using a long match or taper and leave for 15 minutes. Spread the coals into an even layer and leave for 40 minutes, or until they are covered with a thin layer of gray ash and are hot enough to start cooking. Spread the hot coals at least 1 inch/2.5 cm further than the area on which you will be cooking the food.

Never add petrol, lighter fluid, or other flammable materials to a barbecue.

4 To control the heat of the barbecue once the coals are hot enough for cooking, raise or lower the grill rack. If your barbecue has air vents, open these to raise the temperature of the barbecue and close them to lower it. You can also push the hot coals carefully into the center of the barbecue to provide a higher heat in the middle and a lower heat nearer the edges, where you can put food once it is cooked.

safety

Barbecuing is a safe way of cooking as long as you use your common sense. Try not to be over-ambitious if you have not used a barbecue before and always err on the side of caution.

- Make sure that your barbecue is stable and on a flat surface before you light it. Once it is lit, do not move it.
- Keep the barbecue away from trees and shrubs and cut back a shrub instead of moving the barbecue. Note which way the wind is blowing before lighting the barbecue.
- Never add any flammable liquids to try to speed up the ignition of the barbecue. Only ever use fuels designed for the purpose, such as firelighter cubes and liquid. Remember that some fuels take time to build up heat.
- Use only the recommended types of fuel on your barbecue, following any instructions that came with it. Some fuels are not appropriate for some types of barbecue.
- Always have a bucket of water nearby in case the fire gets out of control. If your barbecue has a lid, this will also help to control the flames.
- Fat dripping from meat will make the coals flare up and can cause flames to get out of control. Trim excess fats from meats and shake or scrape off any excess marinade before adding to the barbecue.
- To avoid salmonella, listeria, and food poisoning, always make sure that meat is cooked through. Pay attention in particular to chicken, turkey, pork, and sausages. The cooked meat should have no pink flesh and the juices should run clear (not pink) when the meat is pierced through the thickest part with a skewer or the tip of a sharp knife.

- If it is a particularly hot day, keep perishable foods in the refrigerator until it is time to serve them. Alternatively, you can store them outside in a cool bag with ice packs. Foods that can go off quickly and make people ill include meat, yogurt, and mayonnaise.
- Do not reheat poultry once it has cooled. This rule includes putting food back on the barbecue if it has cooled down. When you serve your meal, try to make sure that the meat is thoroughly cooked through; if not, return to a hot barbecue before it cools down.
- Keep salads and cooked foods away from raw meat and wash your hands carefully after handling raw meat. Use different cutting boards, serving plates, and utensils for raw meats.
- Keep pets away from food and the barbecue to avoid contamination and accidents. Cover food with netting or clean dish towels to keep insects away. Do not use the same dish towel to cover raw meat, then salad.
- Keep children away from the barbecue and teach them about the dangers of playing too close. Always have another adult nearby to supervise the children when you are cooking.
- Do not use a barbecue when you have been drinking alcohol and keep any strong alcoholic drinks away from the barbecue, as they can be flammable.
- Use utensils with long handles and make sure you have a range of tools handy so you do not leave the barbecue unattended. Keep oven mitts nearby.

tools and equipment

Oven mitts are useful to have, as the barbecue may become very hot after a while. Kabob skewers can burn your fingers, even if they are made of wood or bamboo. Plastic utensils should be avoided, as the intense heat from the barbecue can melt them. Metal utensils are best, but remember that they can get very hot. Buy good-quality utensils—a range of different ones will be useful, especially long-handled spoons, forks, and spatulas

designed specifically for barbecues. Include a pair of tongs, a brush, or spoon for basting meat, and something for scraping stuck-on marinades and pieces of food off the grill. If you are using kabob skewers, metal ones can be rubbed with a piece of paper towel with some oil on it to stop the food from sticking. Bamboo and wooden skewers should be soaked in cold water for at least 30 minutes before using to prevent them burning. Wire fish baskets are useful extras, as they enable you to turn whole fish without the risk of it breaking up. They are available in a variety of styles and sizes. Brush with oil before using.

barbecue foods

You can start by cooking a basic barbecue with traditional ingredients, such as sausages, hamburgers, drumsticks, chops, and steaks. Simple foods like these are often best for children and large groups. Sausages are usually quite fatty, so prick them with a fork before cooking to stop them splitting, but watch for too much fat running onto the hot coals and causing flames to shoot up. Hamburgers can be made easily at home. You should prepare foods no more than a day before you are going to cook them, although foods such as hamburgers and sausages can be frozen. Thaw all meats thoroughly before cooking.

Steaks are very easy to cook and many guests will enjoy cooking their own. However, do make sure there are not too many people round the barbecue. Trim off any visible fat from the steak before cooking, as this will make it healthier and stop the fat from dripping onto the hot coals. Chops should be prepared in the same way and need to be cooked for quite a long time, especially if they have a bone. Pork chops should be especially well cooked—15–20 minutes for a chop 1-inch/2.5-cm thick—and check to make sure that they are cooked through.

Many different types of fish can be cooked on a barbecue, from succulent salmon or tuna steaks to whole sardines and mackerel fillets. If you are going to cook fish steaks, select cuts that are of a uniform thickness, as these will cook more evenly. Try salmon steaks sprinkled with lemon juice and herbs or served with dill butter. Fish steaks have a tendency to fall apart and are often best cooked in foil packages, which keep them moist and protect them from burning. Fish kabobs work very well, but be sure to choose a fish, such as cod or angler fish, that will hold together well —there is nothing more annoying than watching your food break apart and disappear into the coals at the bottom of the barbecue. Cod is ideal for kabobs and will go well with a strongly flavored or spicy marinade. Oily fish, such as sardines or mackerel, will cook well on the barbecue and will not dry out.

Remember to be careful about washing your hands and cooking utensils between handling raw meats and other ingredients—for example, do not add a pat of butter to cooking chicken and use the same knife to spread butter on a bread roll. Remember to use separate cutting boards for meat and vegetables and do not put cooked meat near raw meat. Store foods out of direct sunlight and keep them chilled for as long as possible before cooking. Be especially aware when cooking food for young children, pregnant women, or the elderly, as they are particularly susceptible to food poisoning, which can have serious effects. Chicken and raw eggs may contain salmonella, and mayonnaise and other egg-based dressings should be treated as carefully as raw meat.

cooking times

It is difficult to give precise times for cooking food on the barbecue, but this guide offers a rough idea. Before you start cooking, you should make sure that the barbecue is very hot and that the grill rack is at the correct height. An easy way to gauge the heat is to hold out your hand slightly above the grill rack. If you can keep it there for only 2–3 seconds, the barbecue is hot enough to sear meat—any longer and it is not hot enough. Most foods, such as steaks and burgers, will need to be turned once or twice during cooking, but sausages and kabobs need to be turned frequently to ensure that they are evenly cooked. Do not leave food cooking unattended.

beef

- Steaks 1-inch/2.5-cm thick should be cooked over hot coals for 8 minutes. Cook for 5 minutes if you prefer steak rare, and for 12 minutes if you prefer it well done.
- Burgers ¾-inch/2-cm thick should be cooked over hot coals for 6–8 minutes.
- Kabobs made with medium-size pieces of beef should be cooked for 7 minutes over hot coals.

lamb

- Leg steaks should be cooked over medium hot coals for 10–15 minutes. If they are thicker than ¾ inch/ 2 cm, increase the cooking time or use a meat mallet to tenderize and flatten them a little.
- Chops 1-inch/2.5-cm thick are best cooked over medium hot coals for 15 minutes.
- Kabobs made with 1-inch/2.5-cm cubes of lamb should be cooked for about 8–15 minutes over medium hot coals.

pork

- Cook chops for 15–20 minutes over medium hot coals and make sure that they are cooked through. If they are thicker than 1 inch/2.5 cm, increase the cooking time accordingly.
- Kabobs made with 1-inch/2.5-cm cubes of pork should be cooked for about 15 minutes over medium hot coals.
- Most pork spareribs are quite thick and will need to be cooked over medium hot coals for 40 minutes to ensure that they are cooked thoroughly.
- Thick sausages will need 10 minutes over medium hot coals; thinner ones may be ready slightly earlier.

chicken

- Quarters, legs, and breasts with a bone should be cooked for 35 minutes over medium hot coals.
- Cook chicken drumsticks for 25–35 minutes over medium hot coals until the juices run clear, not pink, when you pierce the thickest part of the leg with a skewer or the tip of a knife. If the drumsticks are very large, increase the cooking time.
- Whole breasts will need to be cooked over medium to hot coals for 15–20 minutes.
- Kabobs made with 1-inch/2.5-cm cubes of chicken should be cooked through after 10 minutes over medium hot coals.

fish and seafood

- Whole large fish can be cooked on a barbecue, if cooked over a low to medium heat. Allow 10 minutes per 1-inch/2.5-cm thickness.
- Cook whole small fish, up to 2 lb/900 g, for 14–20 minutes over medium to hot coals.
- Whole sardines should be cooked over medium to hot coals for 5–7 minutes.
- Fish steaks, such as salmon or tuna, or fish fillets up to 1-inch/2.5-cm thick, should be cooked for 6–10 minutes over medium hot coals.
- Fish kabobs made with 1-inch/2.5-cm cubes of fish should be cooked over medium hot coals for 7 minutes.
- Shrimp in their shells should be cooked over medium hot coals for 7 minutes if they are large. Smaller shrimp should be threaded onto kabob skewers. Large shelled shrimp will cook slightly faster.
- Scallops or mussels in their shells should be cooked over medium hot coals until they open. Discard any scallops or mussels that do not open. Shelled and skewered seafood should be cooked for 7 minutes over medium hot coals.

spit-roasting

If you are lucky enough to have a roasting spit on your barbecue, you will find it invaluable when cooking for large numbers of guests. If you have parties regularly in summer and already have a barbecue, you will save time and effort by spit-roasting dishes. You can just put the meat on the spit and let it cook, while you spend most of your time with your guests. If you have a large family, a roasting spit can offer a healthy and filling alternative to a roast dinner. Baste the meat frequently while it is cooking to ensure an evenly cooked and succulent result.

- Joints of beef, such as rump or sirloin, up to about 3 lb 5 oz/1.5 kg will cook very well on a spit and will take 2–3 hours, depending on their size.
- A rolled shoulder of lamb weighing about 3 lb 5 oz/1.5 kg will cook in 1–1½ hours, depending on how well done you like it.
- Shoulder or loin joints of pork weighing about 3 lb 5 oz/1.5 kg will take 2–3 hours to cook through. Test with a skewer or the tip of a sharp knife.
- Whole chickens weighing up to 3 lb 5 oz/1.5 kg will take 1¼ hours to cook. Test with a skewer or the tip of a sharp knife, as they can take longer.
- Whole ducklings weighing up to 5 lb/2.25 kg are very fatty and take 1–1½ hours to cook.

hints and tips

The key to a successful barbecue is planning. It helps to know roughly how many people are coming, but if you are expecting a large number of guests, without knowing how many, make a good supply of basics, such as burgers, to be sure everyone has enough to eat. Most dishes freeze well and you can cook them under a conventional broiler when you need them later.

You can make dishes for your barbecue well in advance. Make and freeze sausages, kabobs, and burgers, although fish kabobs tend not to freeze well. Remove from the freezer 24 hours in advance and thaw in the refrigerator. Make salads in the morning, but avoid chopping ingredients that bruise or brown, such as avocado. Add dressings just before serving or put in a bowl at the table, as adding them to your salads too early will cause them to go soggy.

When you have lit the barbecue, you can start to bring the meat outside. Brush the grill rack with a little corn oil to stop food sticking, being careful not to drip too much oil onto the hot coals.

Don't try to cook too much on the grill rack at once, as the food will not cook through or evenly. Try to cook the same types of food at the same time to avoid contamination. The coals should cover an area wider than that of the food, so even the edges of the grill rack should be quite hot. Use the edges to cook foods that require a lower heat to save having to let the barbecue cool down.

If you are cooking for vegetarian guests as well as meat-eaters, you may have to think about your barbecue a little more carefully. Vegetarian dishes should not be cooked on the same grill as meat dishes—you can keep a separate grill for vegetarians, although it is not fair to expect them to wait until everybody else's food is ready. You could also buy a disposable barbecue to cook only vegetable dishes. The easiest solution is to serve vegetarians with foil packages of mixed beans, vegetables, and cheese with a dressing. These packages keep foods separate during cooking, can be cooked on the same grill as meat and are delicious. You could make a lot of these and serve them to meat-eaters as a side dish. For vegetarians, provide a choice of foods such as a selection of kabobs, packages, salads, and baked potatoes.

Foil packages are often the best solution for cooking desserts. The simplest dessert and one popular with children is marshmallows toasted over the cooling coals, but this must be closely supervised. You can buy a disposable barbecue or use a separate rack, but wash utensils that have been used for savory dishes.

Try to plan the menu so that there is something for everyone. There may be vegetarian guests, fussy children, or meat-eaters not keen on salads, so offer a range of dishes. Remember to have a main vegetable to go with meat or fish. Foil-wrapped baked potatoes cooked on the barbecue are the easiest. Preheat the oven to 400°F/200°C and cook the potatoes for 30 minutes, before transferring to the barbecue, as they can take a long time to cook. Fresh bread rolls are also a good idea.

Offer a choice of drinks, alcoholic and non-alcoholic. Fruit punch with little or no alcohol is usually popular. The person cooking should drink only a very small amount of alcohol, as a drunken cook can be a dangerous one. Watch out for other adults who have been drinking and want to cook.

Remember to keep small children away from the barbecue and warn them about sharp knives and skewers.

Even if a shower of rain interrupts your barbecue, the party can continue—to keep cooking, just pull the lid over the barbecue and open its air vents. Alternatively, take the prepared food inside and carry on cooking under the broiler in your kitchen. When the rain stops, the party can move back into the garden!

basic recipes

marinades

Not only do marinades tenderize and flavor ingredients, but they can be brushed on the food as it is cooking to keep it moist and succulent. As a rule, the longer you can leave food to marinate, the better—overnight in the refrigerator is usually ideal. The exception is citrus marinades with fish, as lemon, lime, or orange juice starts to "cook" the fish after about 1 hour.

Mix the marinade and pour it over the ingredients in a shallow, nonmetallic dish. Turn the ingredients in the marinade to ensure that they are evenly coated, then cover with plastic wrap. Leave the dish in a cool place, rather than the refrigerator, if you are marinating for a short time—up to 1 hour.

Drain the food before cooking, even if you intend to brush it with the marinade. Otherwise, the marinade will drip on the hot coals and may cause them to flare up dangerously. Let the food to come to room temperature before cooking. If you plan to serve leftover marinade as a sauce with the cooked food, bring it to a boil first to prevent bacterial infection. Better still, set aside some of the mixture in advance so that it never comes into contact with raw meat, poultry, or fish.

Allow about ⅔ cup marinade to every 1 lb/450 g of food.

red wine marinade

⅔ cup red wine
1 tbsp olive oil
1 tbsp red wine vinegar
1 tbsp whole-grain mustard
2 bay leaves, torn or crumbled
2 garlic cloves, finely chopped
pepper

yogurt marinade

4 tbsp plain yogurt
1 tbsp olive oil
1 tbsp balsamic vinegar
1 tbsp Dijon mustard
8 fresh sage leaves, finely chopped
ground white pepper

hot pepper marinade

5 tbsp tomato paste
4 tbsp lime juice
1 tbsp red wine vinegar
2 tsp honey
1 tsp Tabasco sauce
1 tsp ground allspice
pepper

white wine marinade

⅔ cup dry white wine
4 tbsp olive oil
1 tbsp lemon juice
3 tbsp finely chopped fresh parsley
1 garlic clove, finely chopped
pepper

sauces and dressings

Many sauces can be made in advance and are a simple way to turn a chop, burger, or drumstick into something special.

mild mustard sauce

2 egg yolks
2 tbsp lemon juice
2 garlic cloves, chopped
1¼ cups olive oil
1 tbsp Dijon mustard
salt and pepper

1 Place the egg yolks, lemon juice, and garlic in a food processor and process until blended and smooth. With the motor still running, gradually add the olive oil through the feeder tube until thick and creamy.

2 Transfer to a bowl, stir in the mustard, and season to taste with salt and pepper.

guacamole

2 avocados
3 scallions, finely chopped
1 garlic clove, finely chopped
2 fresh green chiles, seeded and finely chopped
2 tbsp olive oil

4 tbsp lime juice
salt
chopped fresh cilantro, to garnish

1 Halve and pit the avocados, then scoop the flesh into a bowl. Coarsely mash the avocado flesh with a fork, then stir in the scallions, garlic, chiles, olive oil, and lime juice. Season to taste with salt and sprinkle the chopped cilantro on top.

mayonnaise

⅔ cup corn oil
⅔ cup olive oil
2 egg yolks
salt and pepper
1 tbsp white wine vinegar
2 tsp Dijon mustard

1 Mix the oils together in a pitcher. Beat the egg yolks with a pinch of salt. Gradually add the oil, a drop at a time, beating constantly with a whisk or electric mixer. When one-quarter of the oil has been incorporated, beat in the vinegar. Continue adding the oil, in a steady stream, beating constantly until it is all incorporated and the mixture is thick and creamy. Stir in the mustard and season to taste with salt and pepper.

> **variation**
>
> To make lemon mayonnaise, substitute lemon juice for the white wine vinegar and 1 tablespoon of chopped fresh lemon thyme for the mustard.

fish & seafood

Barbecuing fish gives it a uniquely delicious flavor, but it can be quite tricky to do well, as the fierce heat of the coals can dry out the delicate flesh of even oily fish. This chapter is packed with clever ideas for protecting the texture and simultaneously enhancing the flavor of a wide variety of fish and seafood.

Wrapping fish in a foil pocket, as in Cod & Tomato Packages (see page 24) is a popular way to barbecue it, keeping it moist and sealing in the flavor. However, there are lots of other, more interesting kinds of wraps, too, from Bacon-Wrapped Trout (see page 28) to Mackerel in a Lettuce Jacket (see page 34) and Thai-style banana leaves for Baked Red Snapper (see page 32). Marinades, ranging from refreshing combinations of citrus juice and herbs to fiery mixtures of chile and spices, not only add flavor, but can be brushed on the fish while it is cooking to ensure succulent results.

The recipes have been inspired by dishes from round the world and there is sure to be something to suit all tastes and appetites, from Japanese Salmon Teriyaki (see page 19) to Australian Surf & Turf Kabobs (see page 48) and from Caribbean Sea Bass (see page 20) to Greek Red Snapper Packages (see page 33). There are steaks and fillets, whole fish, kabobs, shrimp, scallops, and even oysters. Recipes include inexpensive fish dishes for family lunches, luxurious centerpieces for special occasion barbecues, simple grills for speed and ease, and fabulous sauces and salsas to impress your guests.

caribbean fish kabobs

serves 6   **prep: 10 mins, plus 1 hr marinating**   **cook: 8–10 mins**

Lightly spiced and marinated, these colorful kabobs look and taste delicious. You can use any firm-textured fish, but for an authentic Caribbean flavor, swordfish is perfect.

INGREDIENTS

2 lb 4 oz/1 kg swordfish steaks

3 tbsp olive oil

3 tbsp lime juice

1 garlic clove, finely chopped

1 tsp paprika

salt and pepper

3 onions, cut into wedges

6 tomatoes, cut into wedges

NUTRITIONAL INFORMATION

Calories 274

Protein 32g

Carbohydrate 9g

Sugars 7g

Fat 13g

Saturates 2g

variation

Instead of serving the kabobs with traditional baked potatoes, serve them with baked sweet potatoes.

cook's tip

When using wooden skewers, remember to soak them in a bowl of cold water for 30 minutes, as this prevents them burning during cooking.

1 Using a sharp knife, cut the fish into 1-inch/ 2.5-cm cubes and place in a shallow, nonmetallic dish. Place the oil, lime juice, garlic, and paprika in a measuring cup and mix. Season to taste with salt and pepper. Pour the marinade over the fish, turning to coat. Cover with plastic wrap and let marinate in the refrigerator for 1 hour.

2 Preheat the barbecue. Thread the fish cubes, onion, and tomato wedges alternately onto 6 long, presoaked wooden skewers. Set aside the marinade.

3 Cook the kabobs over medium hot coals for 8–10 minutes, turning and brushing frequently with the reserved marinade. When they

are cooked through, transfer the kabobs to a large serving plate, and serve immediately.

salmon with mango salsa

serves 4

prep: 15 mins, plus 10 mins standing

cook: 6–8 mins

Although an oily fish, salmon can dry out easily on the fierce heat of the barbecue. Make sure that it is well coated with the citrus juice before you start cooking.

INGREDIENTS

4 salmon steaks, about 6 oz/175 g each

finely grated rind and juice
of 1 lime or ½ lemon

salt and pepper

SALSA

1 large mango, peeled,
seeded, and diced

1 red onion, finely chopped

2 passion fruit

2 fresh basil sprigs

2 tbsp lime juice

salt

NUTRITIONAL INFORMATION	
Calories 360	
Protein 37g	
Carbohydrate 11g	
Sugars 9g	
Fat 20g	
Saturates 3g	

cook's tip

The quickest way to dice the mango is to cut it away from the seed in two halves, slice the flesh in a lattice pattern without cutting through the skin, then turn it inside out and cut away the cubes.

1 Preheat the barbecue. Rinse the salmon steaks under cold running water, pat dry with paper towels and place in a large, shallow, nonmetallic dish. Sprinkle with the lime rind and pour the juice over them. Season to taste with salt and pepper, cover and let stand while you make the salsa.

2 Place the mango flesh in a bowl with the onion. Cut the passion fruit in half and scoop out the seeds and pulp with a teaspoon into the bowl. Tear the basil leaves and add them to the bowl with the lime juice. Season to taste with salt and stir. Cover with plastic wrap and set aside until required.

3 Cook the salmon steaks over medium hot coals for 3–4 minutes on each side. Serve immediately with the salsa.

salmon teriyaki

cook: 10 mins

prep: 10 mins, plus 2 hrs marinating

serves 4

This sweet but piquant Japanese-style teriyaki sauce complements the richness of salmon superbly. Choose some really crisp salad greens, such as romaine or iceberg, to serve with the warm sauce.

NUTRITIONAL INFORMATION

Calories 426

Protein 34g

Carbohydrate 22g

Sugars 10g

Fat 21g

Saturates 4g

INGREDIENTS

4 salmon fillets, about 6 oz/175 g each

SAUCE

1 tbsp cornstarch

½ cup dark soy sauce

4 tbsp mirin or medium-dry sherry

2 tbsp rice or cider vinegar

2 tbsp honey

TO SERVE

½ cucumber

mixed salad greens, torn into pieces

4 scallions, thinly sliced diagonally

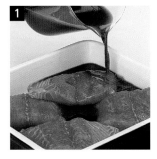

variation

Replace the salmon with 4 x 4 oz/115 g chicken breast portions. Cut slashes in the meat before marinating and cook for about 15 minutes.

1 Rinse the salmon fillets under cold running water, pat dry with paper towels, and place in a large, shallow, nonmetallic dish. To make the sauce, mix the cornstarch and soy sauce in a measuring cup until a paste forms, then stir in the remaining ingredients. Pour three-quarters of the sauce over the salmon, turning to coat. Cover with plastic wrap and let marinate in the refrigerator for 2 hours.

2 Preheat the barbecue. Cut the cucumber into thin sticks, then arrange the salad greens, cucumber, and scallions on 4 serving plates. Pour the remaining sauce into a pan and set over the barbecue to warm through.

3 Remove the salmon fillets from the dish and set aside the marinade. Cook the salmon over medium hot coals, brushing frequently with the reserved marinade, for 3–4 minutes on each side. Transfer the salmon fillets to the prepared serving plates and pour the warmed sauce over them. Serve immediately.

caribbean sea bass

cook: 20 mins   **prep: 15 mins**   **serves 6**

NUTRITIONAL INFORMATION

Calories 211

Protein 36g

Carbohydrate 0g

Sugars 0g

Fat 7g

Saturates 1g

variation

Substitute grapefruit and orange slices for the lemon and lime slices in the fish cavity and use oranges wedges to garnish.

This is a magnificent dish to form the centerpiece of a special occasion barbecue and is surprisingly easy to prepare. A fish basket is essential, as it is almost impossible to turn the fish without breaking it up and spoiling its spectacular appearance.

INGREDIENTS

3 lb 5 oz/1.5 kg sea bass, cleaned and scaled

1–2 tsp olive oil

1 tsp saffron powder

salt and pepper

½ lemon, sliced, plus extra to garnish

1 lime, sliced, plus extra to garnish

1 bunch of fresh thyme

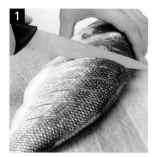

cook's tip

You can sprinkle a few sprigs of dried thyme over the hot coals while you are cooking the fish for extra aroma. Add them toward the end of cooking as they burn very quickly.

1 Preheat the barbecue. Rinse the sea bass inside and out under cold running water, then pat dry with paper towels. Using a sharp knife, make a series of shallow diagonal slashes along each side of the fish. Brush each slash with a little olive oil, then sprinkle over the saffron powder.

2 Brush a large fish basket with olive oil and place the fish in the basket, but do not close it. Season the cavity with salt and pepper. Place the lemon and lime slices and the thyme in the cavity without overfilling it.

3 Close the basket and cook the fish over medium hot coals for 10 minutes on each side. Carefully transfer to a large serving plate, garnish with lemon and lime slices, and serve immediately.

stuffed sardines

serves 6 | **prep: 20 mins, plus 1 hr marinating** | **cook: 6–8 mins**

Barbecued fresh sardines are always a popular choice. They are usually just plainly grilled, but here they are filled with herbs and coated in a mild spice mixture.

INGREDIENTS

1 tbsp fresh parsley, finely chopped	scant ⅔ cup all-purpose flour
4 garlic cloves, finely chopped	1 tsp ground cumin
12 fresh sardines, cleaned and scaled	salt and pepper
3 tbsp lemon juice	olive oil, for brushing

NUTRITIONAL INFORMATION

Calories	327
Protein	36g
Carbohydrate	12g
Sugars	1g
Fat	16g
Saturates	5g

variation

If you like, substitute the chopped fresh parsley with the same amount of chopped fresh dill or thyme.

cook's tip

To clean sardines, slit open the belly and remove the insides. Rinse the cavity and pat dry. To scale, hold the fish by the tail under cold running water and run your other hand along the body from tail to head.

1 Place the parsley and garlic in a bowl and mix together. Rinse the fish inside and out under cold running water and pat dry with paper towels. Spoon the herb mixture into the fish cavities and pat the remainder all over the outside of the fish. Sprinkle the sardines with lemon juice and transfer to a large, shallow, nonmetallic dish. Cover with plastic wrap and let marinate in the refrigerator for 1 hour.

2 Preheat the barbecue. Mix the flour and ground cumin together in a bowl, then season to taste with salt and pepper. Spread out the seasoned flour on a large plate and gently roll the sardines in the flour to coat.

3 Brush the sardines with olive oil and cook over medium hot coals for 3–4 minutes on each side. Serve immediately.

cod & tomato packages

cook: 6–10 mins **prep: 10 mins** serves 4

NUTRITIONAL INFORMATION

Calories 173

Protein 31g

Carbohydrate 3g

Sugars 3g

Fat 3g

Saturates 1g

variation

Beat 4 oz/115 g softened butter and 2 crushed garlic cloves together, then spread on top of the cod steaks in the packages and cook as in main recipe.

Cooking cod steaks in this way keeps the flesh deliciously moist and succulent and seals in the flavor of the herbed tomatoes. White wine gives the packages an added richness.

INGREDIENTS

4 cod steaks, about 6 oz/175 g each

2 tsp extra virgin olive oil

4 tomatoes, peeled and chopped

2 tbsp fresh basil leaves, torn into small pieces

4 tbsp white wine

salt and pepper

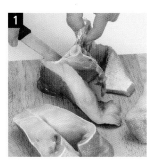

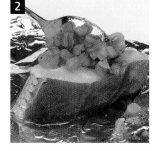

cook's tip

For an attractive presentation, unwrap the packages and slide the contents, tomato side upward, onto serving plates. Remove and discard the skin from the outside of the cod steaks before serving.

1 Preheat the barbecue. Rinse the cod steaks under cold running water and pat dry with paper towels. Using a sharp knife, cut out and discard the central bones. Cut out 4 rectangles, 13 x 8 inches/33 x 20 cm, from double-thickness foil and brush with the olive oil. Place a cod steak in the center of each piece of foil.

2 Mix the tomatoes, basil, and white wine together in a bowl and season to taste with salt and pepper. Spoon the tomato mixture equally on top of the fish. Bring up the sides of the foil and fold over securely.

3 Cook the cod packages over hot coals for 3–5 minutes on each side.

Transfer to 4 large serving plates and serve immediately in the packages.

orange & lemon peppered angler fish

serves 6　　　**prep: 25 mins, plus** ⏱　　　**cook: 20–25 mins** 🕒
1 hr marinating

*Although angler fish appears quite expensive, there is very little
wastage as, apart from the central backbone, the entire tail
is edible. Its flavor is meaty and succulent.*

INGREDIENTS

2 oranges	salt
2 lemons	2 tbsp green peppercorns,
2 angler fish tails, about 1 lb 2 oz/	lightly crushed
500 g each, skinned and cut into	
4 fillets	GARNISH
6 fresh lemon thyme sprigs	orange wedges
2 tbsp olive oil	lemon wedges

NUTRITIONAL INFORMATION

Calories 154

Protein 25g

Carbohydrate 5g

Sugars 5g

Fat 4g

Saturates 1g

variation

If you like, you can substitute the
green peppercorns with either black,
pink, or even mixed peppercorns.

cook's tip

To crush the peppercorns,
place them in a plastic bag
and, using a rolling pin, lightly
crush them. Alternatively, place
them in a mortar and crush
with a pestle, or grind in a
clean coffee mill.

1 Cut 8 orange slices
and 8 lemon slices,
reserving the remaining fruit.
Rinse the angler fish fillets
under cold running water and
pat dry with paper towels.
Place 1 fillet from each angler
fish tail, cut side up, on a
counter and divide the citrus
slices between them. Top with
the lemon thyme. Reassemble
the tails and tie them securely

together at intervals with
kitchen string or trussing
twine. Place the tails in a large,
shallow, nonmetallic dish.

2 Squeeze the juice from
the remaining fruit and
mix with the olive oil in a
measuring cup. Season to taste
with salt, then spoon the
mixture over the fish. Cover
with plastic wrap and let

marinate in the refrigerator
for up to 1 hour, spooning the
marinade over the fish tails
once or twice.

3 Preheat the barbecue.
Drain the angler fish
tails, reserving the marinade.
Sprinkle the crushed green
peppercorns over the fish,
pressing them in with your
fingers. Cook the angler fish

over medium hot coals, turning
and brushing frequently with
the reserved marinade, for
20–25 minutes. Transfer to
a cutting board, remove and
discard the string, and cut
the angler fish tails into slices.
Serve, garnished with orange
and lemon wedges.

bacon-wrapped trout

serves 4   **prep: 15 mins**   **cook: 10–16 mins**

This classic, pan-fried combination is even more delicious cooked on the barbecue, as the smoky flavor of the bacon becomes more pronounced in contrast to the delicate flesh of the fish.

INGREDIENTS

4 trout, cleaned

4 smoked lean bacon strips, rinded

4 tbsp all-purpose flour

salt and pepper

2 tbsp olive oil

2 tbsp lemon juice

corn salad, to serve

GARNISH

fresh parsley sprigs

lemon wedges

NUTRITIONAL INFORMATION	
Calories 448	
Protein 46g	
Carbohydrate 16g	
Sugars 1g	
Fat 23g	
Saturates 6g	

cook's tip

The most commonly available variety of freshwater trout is rainbow trout. Salmon trout, steel-head trout, brown brown trout would also work well in this recipe.

1 Preheat the barbecue. Rinse the trout inside and out under cold running water and pat dry with paper towels. Stretch the bacon using the back of a heavy, flat-bladed knife.

2 Season the flour with salt and pepper and spread it out on a large, flat plate. Gently roll each trout in the seasoned flour until thoroughly coated. Starting just below the head, wrap a strip of bacon in a spiral along the length of each fish.

3 Brush the trout with olive oil and cook over medium hot coals for 5–8 minutes on each side.

Transfer to 4 large serving plates and drizzle with the lemon juice. Garnish with parsley and lemon wedges, and serve with corn salad.

chargrilled tuna with chili salsa

cook: 20 mins

prep: 15 mins, plus 1 hr marinating

serves 4

A firm fish such as tuna is an excellent choice for barbecues, as it is quite meaty and doesn't break up during cooking. Here it is served with a colorful and spicy chili salsa.

NUTRITIONAL INFORMATION

Calories	337
Protein	. . . . .42g
Carbohydrate	. . . . .5g
Sugars	. . . . .5g
Fat	. . . . .16g
Saturates	. . . . .3g

INGREDIENTS

4 tuna steaks, about 6 oz/175 g each

grated rind and juice of 1 lime

2 tbsp olive oil

salt and pepper

fresh cilantro sprigs, to garnish

CHILI SALSA

2 orange bell peppers

1 tbsp olive oil

juice of 1 lime

juice of 1 orange

2–3 fresh red chiles, seeded and chopped

pinch of cayenne pepper

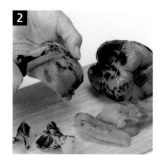

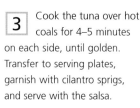

cook's tip

You can make the chili salsa in advance. Cook the bell peppers, skin-side upward, under a preheated hot broiler until blackened and charred, then continue as in Step 2.

1 Rinse the tuna thoroughly under cold running water and pat dry with paper towels, then place in a large, shallow, nonmetallic dish. Sprinkle the lime rind and juice and the olive oil over the fish. Season to taste with salt and pepper, cover with plastic wrap, and let marinate in the refrigerator for up to 1 hour.

2 Preheat the barbecue. To make the salsa, brush the bell peppers with the olive oil and cook over hot coals, turning frequently, for 10 minutes, or until the skin is blackened and charred. Remove from the barbecue and let cool slightly, then remove the skins and discard the seeds. Put the bell peppers into a food processor with the remaining salsa ingredients and process to a purée. Transfer to a bowl and season to taste with salt and pepper.

3 Cook the tuna over hot coals for 4–5 minutes on each side, until golden. Transfer to serving plates, garnish with cilantro sprigs, and serve with the salsa.

serves 4　　**prep: 15 mins, plus 1 hr** ⏲
30 mins cooling/marinating

cook: 55 mins 🍳

This spicy, Mexican-style tuna is sure to be a favorite with your adult guests. The mouthwatering, hot flavors of cayenne, chili, and paprika are given an added twist with a dash of tequila.

INGREDIENTS

4 tuna steaks, about 6 oz/175 g each

fresh cilantro sprigs, to garnish

lime wedges, to serve

SAUCE

2 tbsp corn oil

2 shallots, finely chopped

1 garlic clove, finely chopped

1 red bell pepper, seeded and chopped

2 beefsteak tomatoes, chopped

3 tbsp tomato ketchup

2 tbsp mild mustard

2 tbsp brown sugar

1 tbsp Mexican honey

1 tbsp cayenne pepper

1 tbsp chili powder

1 tbsp paprika

1 tbsp tequila

NUTRITIONAL INFORMATION	
Calories 410	
Protein 44g	
Carbohydrate 25g	
Sugars 24g	
Fat 15g	
Saturates 3g	

variation

This recipe also works well with other oily fish, such as sea trout or salmon. Replace the lime wedges with lemon, if you prefer.

cook's tip

Fresh tuna is meaty and delicious, and is available all year round. Make sure you choose fresh steaks by looking for firm flesh with a bright reddish-pink color.

1 To make the sauce, heat the oil in a heavy-bottom pan. Add the shallots and garlic, and cook over low heat, stirring occasionally, for 5 minutes, or until softened, but not colored. Add the red bell pepper and cook for 1 minute, then add the tomatoes and let simmer, stirring occasionally, for 20 minutes. Stir in the tomato ketchup, mustard, sugar, honey, cayenne, chili powder, paprika, and tequila and let simmer for 20 minutes. Remove the pan from the heat and let cool.

2 Spoon the sauce into a food processor and process to a smooth purée. Rinse the fish under cold running water and pat dry with paper towels. Brush both sides of the tuna fillets with the sauce, place in a shallow dish, cover with plastic wrap, and let marinate in the refrigerator for 1 hour. Set aside the remaining sauce.

3 Preheat the barbecue. Brush the tuna steaks with the sauce and cook over medium hot coals, brushing frequently with the sauce, for 3 minutes on each side. Transfer to serving plates, garnish with fresh cilantro sprigs, and serve immediately with lime wedges.

baked red snapper

serves 4　　　　**prep: 25 mins**　　　　**cook: 15–20 mins**

Banana leaves are the authentic wrapping used in this Indonesian dish. They are available in Asian markets—if you buy them frozen, thaw them before use. Alternatively, wrap the fish in foil.

INGREDIENTS

4 banana leaves

2 limes

3 garlic cloves

4 red snapper, about 12 oz/350 g each

2 scallions, thinly sliced

1-inch/2.5-cm piece fresh gingerroot

1 onion, finely chopped

4½ tsp peanut or corn oil

3 tbsp kecap manis or light soy sauce

1 tsp ground coriander

1 tsp ground cumin

¼ tsp ground cloves

¼ tsp ground turmeric

NUTRITIONAL INFORMATION	
Calories 233
Protein 32g
Carbohydrate 3g
Sugars 1g
Fat 10g
Saturates 0g

cook's tip

Kecap manis is a thick, sweet, Indonesian variety of soy sauce and is available in Asian markets. If you cannot find it, then use light soy sauce instead.

1 Preheat the barbecue. If necessary, cut the banana leaves into 4 x 16-inch/40-cm squares, using a sharp knife or scissors. Thinly slice ½ a lime and 1 garlic clove. Clean and scale the fish, then rinse it inside and out under cold running water. Pat dry with paper towels. Using a sharp knife, make a series of deep diagonal slashes on the side of each fish, then insert the lime and garlic slices into the slashes. Place the fish on the banana leaf squares and sprinkle with the scallions.

2 Finely chop the remaining garlic and squeeze the juice from the remaining limes. Finely chop the ginger, then place the garlic in a bowl with the onion, ginger, oil, kecap manis, spices, and lime juice, and mix to a paste.

3 Spoon the paste into the fish cavities and spread it over the outside. Roll up the packages and tie securely with string. Cook over medium hot coals, turning occasionally, for 15–20 minutes. Serve.

greek red snapper packages

cook: 16–20 mins

prep: 20 mins, plus 45 mins marinating

serves 4

Although the fish is wrapped in grape leaves, it is worth using a fish basket to ensure that you can turn it during cooking without damage. The grape leaves keep the fish moist and full of flavor.

NUTRITIONAL INFORMATION	
Calories	364
Protein	33g
Carbohydrate	1g
Sugars	0g
Fat	26g
Saturates	3g

INGREDIENTS

4 red snapper, about 12 oz/350 g each, cleaned and scaled

salt and pepper

4 garlic cloves, thinly sliced

4 tbsp finely chopped mixed fresh chervil, oregano, and rosemary

6 tbsp extra virgin olive oil, plus extra for brushing

2 tbsp red wine vinegar

16–20 grape leaves in brine, drained and rinsed in boiling water

cook's tip

If using fresh grape leaves, trim off the stems, place in a pan, and add enough cold water to cover. Bring to a boil, then drain immediately and refresh under cold running water.

1 Rinse the fish inside and out under cold running water and pat dry with paper towels. Using a sharp knife, make a series of diagonal slashes along each side of the fish. Season the slashes with salt and pepper and fill with the garlic and herbs. Transfer the fish to a large, shallow, nonmetallic dish. Mix the oil and vinegar together in a measuring cup and season to taste with salt and pepper. Pour the marinade over the fish, then cover with plastic wrap and let marinate in the refrigerator for up to 45 minutes.

2 Preheat the barbecue. Brush a fish basket with olive oil. Wrap the fish in the prepared grape leaves, making sure that the entire body is covered. Transfer the fish to the fish basket.

3 Cook the fish over medium hot coals for 8–10 minutes on each side. Serve immediately.

mackerel in a lettuce jacket

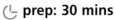

cook: 35 mins   **prep: 30 mins**   **serves 6**

NUTRITIONAL INFORMATION

Calories 582

Protein 45g

Carbohydrate 14g

Sugars 5g

Fat 39g

Saturates 9g

Mackerel has firm-textured flesh with a good flavor. It is very nutritious and makes a filling meal. It is traditionally served with a sharp-tasting sauce, often made with gooseberries, but in this case, they are used as a filling. Serve with new potatoes and salad.

INGREDIENTS

24–30 large romaine or iceberg lettuce leaves

6 mackerel, cleaned

salt and pepper

2 tbsp creamed horseradish

18 fresh dill sprigs

FILLING

½ cup water

2 tbsp lemon juice

1 cooking apple

½ oz/15 g butter

2 shallots, finely chopped

generous ½ cup fresh gooseberries, topped and tailed

½ cup fresh white bread crumbs

½ cup medium oatmeal

1 tbsp hard cider

2 tbsp chopped fresh dill

salt and pepper

variation

You can use canned gooseberries if fresh are unavailable. Alternatively, replace the gooseberries with the same quantity of coarsely chopped rhubarb.

cook's tip

Cook the packages seam-side down first to seal for 5 minutes, then carefully turn the packages over with tongs or a spatula and cook for an additional 5 minutes, or until the fish is tender.

1 Preheat the barbecue. To make the filling, pour the water into a bowl and stir in the lemon juice. Peel, core, and dice the apple and place in the water. Melt the butter in a pan. Add the shallots and cook, stirring occasionally, for 5 minutes, or until softened. Drain the apple, reserving the soaking water, and add to the pan with the

gooseberries. Cook, stirring, for 2–3 minutes, then add the soaking water. Let simmer gently for 5 minutes, until the fruit is tender. Remove from the heat and let cool.

2 Meanwhile, blanch the lettuce leaves in boiling water for 10 seconds, then drain and refresh under cold running water.

3 Mix the bread crumbs, 2 tablespoons of the oatmeal, and the cider in a bowl, then stir into the cooled fruit mixture. Stir in the chopped dill and season to taste with salt and pepper. Rinse the mackerel inside and out under cold running water and pat dry. Season the cavities with salt and pepper and spoon in the filling.

4 Spread 1 teaspoon of horseradish over the fish and coat with the remaining oatmeal. Arrange 4–5 lettuce leaves to form a rectangle and place 3 dill sprigs in the center. Top with a fish and wrap the leaves round to enclose all but the head and tail. Repeat with the other fish. Cook over medium hot coals for 10 minutes on each side. Serve.

mixed seafood brochettes

serves 6 **prep: 15 mins, plus 1 hr marinating** **cook: 20 mins**

Seafood brochettes always look attractive and are perennially popular. Here they are served with a flavorsome sauce for dipping.

INGREDIENTS

2 tbsp sesame seeds	salt and pepper
1 lb 2 oz/500 g swordfish steaks or angler fish fillet	1½ tsp cornstarch
	2 tbsp water
1½ cups dry white wine	2 tbsp chopped fresh cilantro
2 tbsp corn oil	12 prepared scallops
grated rind and juice of 2 limes	12 raw jumbo shrimp
2 garlic cloves, finely chopped	

NUTRITIONAL INFORMATION

Calories 257

Protein 31g

Carbohydrate 5g

Sugars 1g

Fat 9g

Saturates 2g

variation

For a budget dish, replace half the shrimp with tomato wedges and half the scallops with onion wedges. Brush with the marinade during cooking.

cook's tip

Don't shell the shrimp as they look more attractive cooked in their shells. Keep an empty bowl handy for the discarded shrimps' heads and shells.

1 Dry-fry the sesame seeds in a covered heavy-bottom skillet until they start to pop and give off their aroma. Remove from the heat and set aside. Cut the fish into 1-inch/2.5-cm cubes, then place in a shallow, nonmetallic dish. Mix ¾ cup of the wine, the oil, lime rind and juice, and garlic together in a measuring cup and season to taste with salt and pepper. Pour half of this over the fish, turning to coat, and pour the remainder into a small pan. Cover the fish with plastic wrap and let marinate in a cool place or the refrigerator for up to 1 hour.

2 Preheat the barbecue. Set the pan over low heat and add the remaining white wine. Mix the cornstarch and water into a smooth paste and stir it into the pan, then bring to a boil, stirring constantly, and let simmer until thickened. Remove the pan from the heat and stir in the chopped cilantro and roasted sesame seeds. Cover with a lid and place by the side of the barbecue to keep warm.

3 Remove the fish from the marinade and thread onto 6 metal skewers, alternating with the scallops and shrimp. Cook the brochettes over medium hot coals, turning occasionally, for 5–8 minutes, or until the fish is cooked and the shrimp have changed color. Transfer to a large serving plate and serve immediately with the sauce.

indonesian spiced fish

cook: 16 mins

prep: 15 mins, plus 1 hr marinating

serves 6

This exotic barbecued treat looks spectacular and has a flavor to match. Chile, fresh gingerroot, and lime juice are combined in a spicy paste to coat the fish and permeate its flesh before grilling.

NUTRITIONAL INFORMATION	
Calories	183
Protein	27g
Carbohydrate	1g
Sugars	1g
Fat	8g
Saturates	1g

variation

If you like, substitute the corn oil with the same quantity of sunflower-seed oil. You can also replace the lime juice with lemon juice.

INGREDIENTS

2 lb 4 oz/1 kg sea bream or red snapper

4 garlic cloves, finely chopped

2 fresh red chiles, seeded and finely chopped

1-inch/2.5-cm piece fresh gingerroot, thinly sliced

4 scallions, chopped

juice of 1 lime

2 tbsp corn oil, plus extra for brushing

salt

shredded coconut, to garnish (optional)

cook's tip

To clean the fish, use a sharp knife to slit open the belly and remove the innards. When scaling fish, it is best to do it either outside or in a plastic bag as the scales can go everywhere.

1 Clean the fish (see cook's tip), then remove the scales, starting at the tail and working toward the head. Rinse the fish inside and out under cold running water and pat dry with paper towels. Using a sharp knife, make a series of diagonal slashes on both sides of the fish. Place the fish in a large, shallow, nonmetallic dish.

2 Put the garlic, chiles, ginger, and scallions into a food processor and process to a paste. Transfer to a small bowl, stir in the lime juice and oil, and season to taste with salt. Place 1–2 tablespoons of the spice mixture into the cavity of the fish and spoon the remainder over the fish, turning to coat. Cover with plastic wrap and let

marinate in a cool place or the refrigerator for up to 1 hour.

3 Preheat the barbecue. Lightly brush a fish basket with oil and place the fish in it, reserving the marinade. Cook over medium hot coals, basting frequently with the marinade, for 8 minutes on each side, or

until the flesh flakes easily. Serve immediately, garnished with coconut if you like.

sizzling scallops

serves 4   **prep: 10 mins, plus 30 mins marinating**   **cook: 8–10 mins**

This is a new and great way to cook scallops on the barbecue. You can also use other shellfish, such as oysters, if you prefer.

INGREDIENTS

1 lemon

6 tbsp olive oil

salt and pepper

12 prepared scallops

2 cups fresh whole-wheat
bread crumbs

2 oz/55 g butter, melted

lemon wedges, to garnish (optional)

NUTRITIONAL INFORMATION

Calories 432

Protein 26g

Carbohydrate 15g

Sugars 1g

Fat 30g

Saturates 10g

cook's tip

If you like, it is not necessary to cut off the orange coral, if there is any, before coating and cooking the scallops. Leave a small space between each scallop to ensure even cooking.

1 Finely grate the lemon rind, then place it in a dish with the olive oil and mix together. Season to taste. Add the scallops, tossing to coat, then cover and let marinate for 30 minutes.

2 Place the bread crumbs in a large bowl. Add the scallops, one at a time, and toss until they are well coated, then thread onto individual presoaked wooden skewers. Drizzle with the melted butter.

3 Cook the scallops over medium hot coals, turning once, for 8–10 minutes. Transfer to a large serving dish, garnish with lemon wedges, if you like, and serve immediately.

scallops & bacon

cook: 10 mins   **prep: 20 mins**   **serves 4**

These scrumptious nibbles are delicious served piping hot with chilled aïoli and a glass of champagne or sparkling wine.

NUTRITIONAL INFORMATION

Calories 974

Protein 55g

Carbohydrate 5g

Sugars 0g

Fat 82g

Saturates 21g

INGREDIENTS

20 prepared scallops

4 tbsp lemon juice

salt and pepper

20 lean bacon strips, rinded

AIOLI

4 garlic cloves, crushed

salt and pepper

2 egg yolks

1 cup extra virgin olive oil

variation

These bacon-wrapped scallops are also tasty served with tartare sauce, instead of the aïoli.

1 Preheat the barbecue. To make the aïoli, place the garlic in a bowl, add a pinch of salt, and mash with the back of a spoon. Add the egg yolks and beat with an electric whisk for 30 seconds, or until creamy. Beat in the olive oil, one drop at a time. As the mixture starts to thicken, add the oil in a steady stream, beating constantly.

Season to taste with salt and pepper, cover the bowl, and let chill until required.

2 Sprinkle the scallops with the lemon juice and season to taste with salt and pepper. Stretch the bacon strips with a heavy, flat-bladed knife, then wrap a strip round each scallop and secure with toothpicks.

3 Cook the scallops over medium hot coals for 5 minutes on each side. Transfer to a large serving plate and serve immediately with the aïoli.

chargrilled devils

cook: 5 mins **prep: 30 mins** serves 4

NUTRITIONAL INFORMATION

Calories	.444
Protein	.32g
Carbohydrate	.3g
Sugars	.1g
Fat	.34g
Saturates	.13g

variation

You can replace the shallot with a small, finely chopped onion and the fresh parsley with the same amount of snipped fresh chives, if you prefer.

This is a barbecue version of the classic appetizer "angels on horseback," and goes to prove how sophisticated and elegant al fresco dining can be.

INGREDIENTS

36 fresh oysters	1 shallot, finely chopped
18 lean bacon strips, rinded	2 tbsp finely chopped fresh parsley
1 tbsp mild paprika	2 tbsp lemon juice
1 tsp cayenne pepper	salt and pepper

SAUCE
1 fresh red chile, seeded and
finely chopped
1 garlic clove, finely chopped

cook's tip

To shuck an oyster, wrap a dish towel round one hand and grasp the oyster, flat shell uppermost. Prise open with a strong knife, then run the blade around the inside of the shell to sever the muscle.

1 Preheat the barbecue. Open the oysters, catching the juice from the shells in a bowl. Cut the oysters from the bottom shells, set aside, and tip any remaining juice into the bowl. To make the sauce, add the red chile, garlic, shallot, parsley, and lemon juice to the bowl, then season to taste

with salt and pepper and mix well. Cover the bowl with plastic wrap and let chill in the refrigerator until required.

2 Using a sharp knife, cut each bacon strip in half across the center. Season the oysters with paprika and cayenne, then roll each oyster up inside ½ a bacon strip.

Thread 9 wrapped oysters onto 4 presoaked wooden skewers or toothpicks.

3 Cook over hot coals, turning frequently, for 5 minutes, or until the bacon is well browned and crispy. Transfer to a large serving plate and serve immediately with the sauce.

shrimp with citrus salsa

serves 6   **prep: 25 mins**   **cook: 6 mins**

A fruity, herby salsa brings out the flavor of grilled shrimp. It can be prepared in advance of the barbecue, then left in the refrigerator to chill until your guests are ready to eat.

INGREDIENTS

36 large, raw jumbo shrimp
2 tbsp finely chopped fresh cilantro
pinch of cayenne pepper
3–4 tbsp corn oil
fresh cilantro leaves, to garnish
lime wedges, to serve

SALSA
1 orange
1 tart eating apple, peeled, quartered, and cored
2 fresh red chiles, seeded and chopped
1 garlic clove, chopped
8 fresh cilantro sprigs
8 fresh mint sprigs
4 tbsp lime juice
salt and pepper

NUTRITIONAL INFORMATION

Calories 126

Protein 11g

Carbohydrate 5g

Sugars 5g

Fat 7g

Saturates 1g

variation

If you prefer, you can omit the fresh mint from the salsa and add extra cilantro instead.

cook's tip

To devein shrimp, cut a slit along the back and use the tip of the knife to remove the dark intestinal thread. It is not dangerous to eat, but can spoil the flavor.

1 Preheat the barbecue. To make the salsa, peel the orange and cut into segments. Set aside any juice. Put the orange segments, apple quarters, chiles, garlic, cilantro, and mint into a food processor and process until smooth. With the motor running, add the lime juice through the feeder tube. Transfer the salsa to a serving bowl and season to taste with salt and pepper. Cover with plastic wrap and let chill in the refrigerator until required.

2 Using a sharp knife, remove and discard the heads from the shrimp, then remove the shells. Cut along the back of the shrimp and remove the dark intestinal vein (see cook's tip). Rinse the shrimp under cold running water and pat dry with paper towels. Mix the chopped cilantro, cayenne, and corn oil together in a dish. Add the shrimp and toss well to coat.

3 Cook the shrimp over medium hot coals for 3 minutes on each side, or until they have changed color. Transfer to a large serving plate, garnish with fresh cilantro leaves, and serve immediately with lime wedges and the salsa.

coconut shrimp

serves 4 | **prep: 15 mins, plus 1 hr marinating** | **cook: 8 mins**

This classic Thai combination of flavors is perfect with chargrilled shrimp, but would also go well with other fish and seafood.

INGREDIENTS

6 scallions

1¾ cups coconut milk

finely grated rind and juice of 1 lime

4 tbsp chopped fresh cilantro

2 tbsp corn oil

pepper

1 lb 7 oz/650 g raw jumbo shrimp

GARNISH

lemon wedges

fresh cilantro sprigs

NUTRITIONAL INFORMATION	
Calories	.218
Protein	.29g
Carbohydrate	.7g
Sugars	.6g
Fat	.7g
Saturates	.1g

cook's tip

Coconut milk is not the same as the liquid from inside the fresh nut. It is available in cans from supermarkets and Asian markets.

1 Finely chop the scallions and place in a large, shallow, nonmetallic dish with the coconut milk, lime rind and juice, cilantro, and oil. Mix well and season to taste with pepper. Add the shrimp, turning to coat. Cover with plastic wrap and let marinate in the refrigerator for 1 hour.

2 Preheat the barbecue. Drain the shrimp, reserving the marinade. Thread the shrimp onto 8 long metal skewers.

3 Cook the skewers over medium hot coals, brushing with the reserved marinade and turning frequently, for 8 minutes, or until they have changed color. Cook the lemon wedges, skin-side down over medium hot coals, for the last 5 minutes. Serve the shrimp immediately, garnished with the hot lemon wedges and cilantro sprigs.

spanish shrimp

cook: 25 mins   **prep: 20 mins**   **serves 6**

These fresh shrimp are served with a fiery tomato and chili sauce. If you prefer a milder flavor, you can reduce the number of chiles.

NUTRITIONAL INFORMATION	
Calories	175
Protein	12g
Carbohydrate	5g
Sugars	5g
Fat	12g
Saturates	2g

INGREDIENTS

1 bunch of fresh flat-leaf parsley

36 large, raw shrimp, shelled and deveined, tails left on

3–4 tbsp olive oil

lemon wedges, to garnish

SAUCE

6 fresh red chiles

1 onion, chopped

2 garlic cloves, chopped

1 lb 2 oz/500 g tomatoes, chopped

3 tbsp olive oil

pinch of sugar

salt and pepper

cook's tip

To make the shrimp easier to turn, thread them individually onto small, presoaked wooden skewers. Spread the skewers out on the grill rack to ensure that they are evenly cooked.

1 Preheat the barbecue. Chop enough parsley to fill 2 tablespoons and set aside. To make the sauce, seed and chop the chiles, then put into a food processor with the onion and garlic and process until finely chopped. Add the tomatoes and olive oil and process to a purée.

2 Transfer the mixture to a pan set over very low heat, stir in the sugar and season to taste with salt and pepper. Let simmer very gently, without boiling, for 15 minutes. Transfer the sauce to an earthenware bowl and place on the side of the barbecue to keep warm.

3 Rinse the shrimp under cold running water and pat dry on paper towels. Mix the parsley and olive oil in a dish, add the shrimp, and toss well to coat. Cook the shrimp over medium hot coals for 3 minutes on each side, or until they have changed color. Transfer to a plate, garnish

with lemon wedges, and serve with the sauce.

surf & turf kabobs

NUTRITIONAL INFORMATION

Calories	.516
Protein	.50g
Carbohydrate	.23g
Sugars	.18g
Fat	.26g
Saturates	.5g

variation

Other types of vegetables are also suitable for these kabobs, such as strips of bell pepper and pearl onions.

An Australian favorite that offers the best of both worlds—shrimp from the surf and meat from the turf. The different kabobs are each coated with a flavored oil before cooking.

INGREDIENTS

12 raw jumbo shrimp

4 shallots, halved

12 cherry tomatoes

2 tbsp corn oil

½ tsp ground coriander

pepper

STEAK KABOBS

14 oz/400 g rump steak, cut into 1-inch/2.5-cm cubes

4 onions, quartered

8 bay leaves

2 tbsp corn oil

½–¾ tsp chili powder

CHICKEN KABOBS

14 oz/400 g skinless, boneless chicken breasts, cut into 1-inch/2.5-cm cubes

2 zucchinis, thickly sliced

2 fresh pineapple slices, cut into cubes

2 tbsp corn oil

2 tbsp dark soy sauce

2 tbsp red currant jelly

pepper

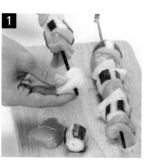

cook's tip

If using metal skewers, brush them with a little oil before threading the pieces of food onto them. This prevents the food sticking to them during cooking.

1 Preheat the barbecue. Remove the heads from the shrimp. Thread the shallots, shrimp, and cherry tomatoes alternately onto 4 metal skewers. Thread the steak, onion quarters, and bay leaves alternately onto 4 metal skewers. Thread the chicken, zucchini slices and pineapple cubes alternately onto 4 metal skewers.

2 For the shrimp kabobs, mix the oil and ground coriander together in a small bowl and season to taste with pepper, then brush all over the kabobs. For the steak kabobs, mix the oil and chili powder to taste in a separate bowl, then brush all over the kabobs. For the chicken kabobs, mix the oil, soy sauce and red currant jelly together in a third bowl and season to taste with pepper, then brush all over the kabobs.

3 Cook the shrimp kabobs over medium hot coals, turning frequently and brushing with any remaining coriander-flavored oil, for 6–8 minutes. Cook the steak kabobs on the hottest part of the barbecue, turning frequently and brushing with any remaining chili-flavored oil, for 5–8 minutes. Cook the chicken kabobs over medium hot coals for 6–10 minutes, turning frequently and brushing with any remaining soy-flavored oil. Serve when the kabobs are all cooked.

poultry

Chicken is one of the most popular barbecue foods and this chapter certainly explores

its dazzling versatility. Whether drumsticks, quarters, breast portions, wings, or kabobs, the

sometimes bland meat is ideal for an immense range of flavorings and marinades. Whether you

like it hot and spicy, subtle and aromatic, rich and full-flavored, or fruity and refreshing, you are

sure to find a chicken dish to set your taste buds tingling. There are familiar favorites, such as

Mustard & Honey Drumsticks (see page 54) and Chicken Tikka (see page 72), as well as some

unusual grills, such as Jamaican Kabobs (see page 56) and Italian Deviled Chicken (see page 70).

Many of the chicken recipes can be easily adapted for cooking turkey breasts

and steaks and this chapter also includes some specific turkey grills, such as tasty little

Turkey Rolls (see page 77), served with colorful red currant relish—a perfect choice for guests.

Duck is an excellent meat for cooking on the barbecue because it is naturally quite fatty.

This ensures that it stays moist. However, for entertaining guests, there is little that is more

impressive than Sage & Lemon Squab Chickens (see page 60)—young chickens that have

been spatchcocked and cooked whole.

As well as marinades, many of the recipes include tasty sauces, salsas, pesto, and tapenades.

Try Drumsticks in a Piquant Dressing (see page 55), Spicy Chicken Wings (see page 68) with a

colorful bell pepper sauce, or Spicy Pita Pockets (see page 74) with a fiery chili sauce. Mix and

match the sauces to suit your family's tastes and to extend your barbecue repertoire.

cajun chicken

cook: 25–30 mins   **prep: 10 mins**   serves 4

NUTRITIONAL INFORMATION

Calories 388

Protein 19g

Carbohydrate 6g

Sugars 1g

Fat 32g

Saturates 15g

Chicken and corn are coated in an aromatic mixture before being blackened—slightly charred—on the barbecue to bring out the many flavors of the different spices.

INGREDIENTS

4 chicken drumsticks

4 chicken thighs

2 fresh corn ears, husks and silks removed

3 oz/85 g butter, melted

1 tsp garlic powder

1 tsp dried thyme

1 tsp cayenne pepper

1 tsp ground black pepper

½ tsp ground white pepper

¼ tsp ground cumin

SPICE MIX

2 tsp onion powder

2 tsp paprika

1½ tsp salt

variation

Try the spice mix on swordfish steaks. Coat the fish and corn separately, then cook the corn for 15 minutes and the fish for 6–8 minutes.

1 Preheat the barbecue. Using a sharp knife, make 2–3 diagonal slashes in the chicken drumsticks and thighs, then place them in a large dish. Cut the corn ears into thick slices and add them to the dish. Mix all the ingredients for the spice mix together in a small bowl.

2 Brush the chicken and corn with the melted butter and sprinkle with the spice mix. Toss to coat well.

3 Cook the chicken over medium hot coals, turning occasionally, for 15 minutes, then add the corn slices and cook, turning occasionally, for an additional 10–15 minutes, or until starting to blacken slightly at the edges. Transfer to a large serving plate and serve immediately.

cook's tip

To remove the husks from the corn ears, gently pull them away from the corn toward the base, then cut off the base and remove the silk.

mustard & honey drumsticks

serves 4   **prep: 10 mins, plus 1 hr marinating**   **cook: 25–30 mins**

Chicken can taste rather bland, but this sweet-and-sour glaze gives it a wonderful piquancy and helps to keep it moist during cooking.

INGREDIENTS

8 chicken drumsticks

fresh parsley sprigs, to garnish

salad, to serve

GLAZE

½ cup honey

4 tbsp Dijon mustard

4 tbsp whole-grain mustard

4 tbsp white wine vinegar

2 tbsp corn oil

salt and pepper

NUTRITIONAL INFORMATION

Calories	.409
Protein	.32g
Carbohydrate	.27g
Sugars	.26g
Fat	.19g
Saturates	.4g

variation

Try this glaze with pork spareribs. Marinate 2 lb/ 900 g spareribs in the glaze for 1 hour. Cook over hot coals, turning frequently and brushing with the glaze, for 15–20 minutes.

1 Using a sharp knife, make 2–3 diagonal slashes in the chicken drumsticks and place them in a large, nonmetallic dish.

2 Mix all the ingredients for the glaze together in a measuring cup and season to taste with salt and pepper. Pour the glaze over the drumsticks, turning until the

drumsticks are well coated. Cover with plastic wrap and let marinate in the refrigerator for at least 1 hour.

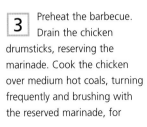

3 Preheat the barbecue. Drain the chicken drumsticks, reserving the marinade. Cook the chicken over medium hot coals, turning frequently and brushing with the reserved marinade, for

25–30 minutes, or until thoroughly cooked. Transfer to serving plates, garnish with fresh parsley sprigs, and serve immediately with salad.

drumsticks in a piquant dressing

⏱ **cook: 2 hrs**   ⏱ **prep: 10 mins, plus 20 mins cooling**   **serves 6**

This tasty dressing gives the chicken drumsticks a rich color as well as a fabulous flavor, which makes them irresistibly appetizing.

NUTRITIONAL INFORMATION	
Calories	266
Protein	31g
Carbohydrate	13g
Sugars	13g
Fat	10g
Saturates	3g

INGREDIENTS

12 chicken drumsticks

DRESSING

1 onion, chopped

1 celery stalk, chopped

1 garlic clove, finely chopped

1 lb 12 oz/800 g canned chopped tomatoes

3 tbsp brown sugar

1 tbsp paprika

¼ tsp Tabasco sauce

1 tbsp Worcestershire sauce

pepper

cook's tip

There are 2 types of paprika—sweet, which is fairly mild tasting, and hot, which is spicier. However, neither type is as hot as cayenne pepper.

1 Preheat the barbecue. To make the dressing, place all the ingredients in a heavy-bottom pan and bring to a boil over low heat. Cover and let simmer gently for 1 hour, or until the onion and celery are very tender. Remove the pan from the heat and let cool.

2 Transfer the dressing to a food processor and process to a purée. Using a metal spoon, gently rub the purée through a fine-meshed strainer into a clean pan and bring to a boil over low heat. Let simmer gently for 25 minutes, or until reduced and thickened.

3 Brush the drumsticks with the sauce and cook over medium hot coals, turning and brushing with the sauce frequently, for 25–30 minutes. Serve. If you wish to serve the remaining sauce with the drumsticks, make sure that it is returned to boiling point first.

jamaican kabobs

serves 4 **prep: 15 mins, plus 1 hr marinating** **cook: 6-10 mins**

What could be better on a hot summer's day than barbecued chicken kabobs flavored with tropical fruit and a dash of rum? Serve with a crisp green salad for a filling barbecue lunch.

INGREDIENTS

2 mangoes

4 skinless, boneless chicken breasts, about 6 oz/175 g each, cut into 1-inch/2.5-cm cubes

finely grated rind and juice of 1 lime

1 tbsp dark rum

1 tbsp brown sugar

1 tsp ground allspice

NUTRITIONAL INFORMATION

Calories 270

Protein 39g

Carbohydrate 15g

Sugars 15g

Fat 6g

Saturates 2g

variation

Try substituting diced turkey breast for the chicken, white wine for the rum, and cinnamon for the allspice.

cook's tip

Make sure that the chicken cubes are all roughly the same size to ensure that they take the same amount of time to cook. Before serving, make sure that they are cooked through.

1. Cut the mango into cubes. Using a sharp knife, cut the flesh from either side of the seed in 2 slices and trim off any flesh still clinging to it. Cut through the flesh in a diamond pattern, but do not cut through the skin. Turn the skin inside out and cut away the cubed flesh. Set aside until required. Place the chicken in a shallow, nonmetallic dish.

Sprinkle the lime rind and juice over the chicken and add the rum, sugar, and allspice. Toss the chicken pieces until well coated, cover with plastic wrap, and let marinate in the refrigerator for 1 hour.

2. Preheat the barbecue. Drain the chicken, reserving the marinade. Thread the chicken pieces and mango cubes alternately onto 8 presoaked wooden skewers.

3. Cook the chicken over medium hot coals, turning and brushing frequently with the marinade, for 6–10 minutes, or until thoroughly cooked. Transfer to a large serving plate and serve immediately.

zesty kabobs

cook: 6–10 mins

prep: 10 mins, plus 8 hrs marinating

serves 4

NUTRITIONAL INFORMATION	
Calories 290	
Protein 38g	
Carbohydrate 10g	
Sugars 10g	
Fat 11g	
Saturates 3g	

These lovely, fresh-tasting chicken kabobs are marinated in a zingy mixture of citrus juice and rind. They are very easy to make and make a perfect main course for a barbecue party.

INGREDIENTS

4 skinless, boneless chicken breasts, about 6 oz/175 g each

finely grated rind and juice of ½ lemon

finely grated rind and juice of ½ orange

2 tbsp honey

2 tbsp olive oil

2 tbsp chopped fresh mint

¼ tsp ground coriander

salt and pepper

GARNISH

fresh mint sprigs

citrus zest

variation

Substitute the lemon rind with the same quantity of lime rind and replace the chopped fresh mint with the same quantity of cilantro or parsley.

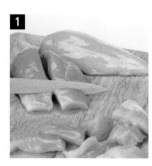

cook's tip

Don't squash the chicken cubes too tightly together on the skewers, otherwise they will not cook evenly and the centers will not properly cook through.

1 Using a sharp knife, cut the chicken into 1-inch/2.5-cm cubes, then place them in a large glass bowl. Place the lemon and orange rind, the lemon and orange juice, the honey, oil, mint, and ground coriander in a measuring cup and mix together. Season to taste with salt and pepper. Pour the marinade over the chicken cubes and toss until thoroughly coated. Cover with plastic wrap and let marinate in the refrigerator for up to 8 hours.

2 Preheat the barbecue. Drain the chicken cubes, reserving the marinade. Thread the chicken onto several long metal skewers.

3 Cook the skewers over medium hot coals, turning and brushing frequently with the reserved marinade, for 6–10 minutes, or until thoroughly cooked. Transfer to a large serving plate, garnish with fresh mint sprigs and citrus zest, and serve immediately.

sage & lemon squab chickens

serves 4 **prep: 30 mins** **cook: 20–30 mins**

Spatchcocked squab chickens are the ideal choice for a barbecue, as they are easy to handle and look attractive. You can buy them ready prepared or spatchcock them yourself.

INGREDIENTS

4 squab chickens, about
1 lb/450 g each
1 lemon
2 tbsp chopped fresh sage
salt and pepper

GARNISH
fresh herb sprigs
lemon slices

NUTRITIONAL INFORMATION	
Calories 375	
Protein 39g	
Carbohydrate 0g	
Sugars 0g	
Fat 24g	
Saturates 7g	

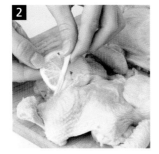
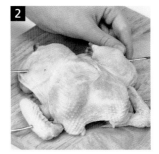

cook's tip

You can thread the skewers crosswise through the squab chicken. Push a skewer through a wing and out through the thigh on the opposite side. Repeat with the other skewer on the other side.

1 Preheat the barbecue. To spatchcock the squab chickens, turn 1 bird breast-side down and, using strong kitchen scissors or poultry shears, cut through the skin and rib cage along both sides of the backbone, from tail to neck. Remove the backbone and turn the bird breast-side up. Press down firmly on the breastbone with the heel of your hand to flatten. Fold the wingtips underneath. Repeat with the remaining squab chickens.

2 Thinly slice half the lemon and finely grate the rind of the other half. Mix the lemon rind and sage together in a small bowl. Loosen the skin on the breasts and legs of the squab chickens and insert the lemon and sage mixture. Tuck in the lemon slices and smooth the skin back firmly. Push a metal skewer through one wing, the top of the breast, and out of the other wing. Push a second skewer through one thigh, the bottom of the breast, and out the other thigh. Season to taste with salt and pepper.

3 Cook the squab chickens over medium hot coals for 10–15 minutes on each side. Serve immediately, garnished with fresh herb sprigs and lemon slices.

jerk chicken

cook: 30–35 mins   **prep: 15 mins, plus 8 hrs marinating**   **serves 4**

Jerk seasoning—a mixture of herbs and spices—is a Jamaican flavoring that was originally used only for pork. It is equally delicious with chicken and this dish is now extremely popular.

NUTRITIONAL INFORMATION

Calories 258

Protein 38g

Carbohydrate 4g

Sugars 3g

Fat 10g

Saturates 2g

INGREDIENTS

2 fresh red chiles

2 tbsp corn oil, plus extra for brushing

2 garlic cloves, finely chopped

1 tbsp finely chopped onion

1 tbsp finely chopped scallion

1 tbsp white wine vinegar

1 tbsp lime juice

2 tsp raw brown sugar

1 tsp dried thyme

1 tsp ground cinnamon

1 tsp ground allspice

¼ tsp freshly grated nutmeg

salt and pepper

4 chicken quarters

cook's tip

For a side dish, trim 2 plantains, cook in a pan of boiling water for 20 minutes, drain and let cool. Peel, cut into thin 2-inch/5-cm pieces, fold in half and thread onto skewers. Oil and cook for 6 minutes.

1 Seed and finely chop the red chiles, then place them in a small glass bowl with the oil, garlic, onion, scallion, vinegar, lime juice, raw brown sugar, thyme, cinnamon, allspice, and nutmeg. Season to taste with salt and pepper and mash thoroughly with a fork.

2 Using a sharp knife, make a series of diagonal slashes in the chicken pieces and place them in a large, shallow, nonmetallic dish. Spoon the jerk seasoning over the chicken, rubbing it well into the slashes. Cover and let marinate in the refrigerator for up to 8 hours.

3 Preheat the barbecue. Remove the chicken from the marinade, discarding the marinade, brush with oil and cook over medium hot coals, turning frequently, for 30–35 minutes. Transfer to plates and serve.

thai chicken

cook: 30–35 mins

prep: 10 mins, plus 8 hrs marinating

serves 4

NUTRITIONAL INFORMATION

Calories 268

Protein 33g

Carbohydrate 9g

Sugars 6g

Fat 11g

Saturates 3g

Roadside stalls serve meals and snacks throughout the day and night in every Thai city. Spicy barbecued chicken is the number one favorite. Serve with a green salad for a delicious barbecue lunch.

INGREDIENTS

4 chicken quarters or 8 chicken pieces

2 lemon grass stalks, coarsely chopped

6 garlic cloves, coarsely chopped

1 bunch scallions, coarsely chopped

1-inch/2.5-cm piece fresh gingerroot, coarsely chopped

½ bunch cilantro roots, coarsely chopped

1 tbsp jaggery

½ cup coconut milk

2 tbsp Thai fish sauce (nam pla)

2 tbsp dark soy sauce

lime wedges, to garnish

variation

To make a sauce, mix 4 tablespoons fish sauce, 2 tablespoons lemon juice, 2 crushed garlic cloves, 1 tablespoon sugar, and 1 tablespoon chili powder.

cook's tip

Jaggery, cilantro roots, coconut milk, and Thai fish sauce are all available from specialist Asian markets. If you cannot find jaggery then use brown sugar instead.

1 Place the chicken in a single layer in a large, shallow, nonmetallic dish. Put the lemon grass, garlic, scallions, ginger, cilantro roots, jaggery, coconut milk, fish sauce, and soy sauce into a food processor and process to a smooth purée. Pour the spice mixture over the chicken, turning until the chicken is thoroughly coated. Cover the dish with plastic wrap and let marinate in the refrigerator for up to 8 hours.

2 Preheat the barbecue. Drain the chicken, reserving the marinade.

3 Cook over medium hot coals, turning and brushing frequently with the reserved marinade, for 30–35 minutes, or until thoroughly cooked. Serve immediately, garnished with lime wedges.

hot red chicken

cook: 25–30 mins

**prep: 10 mins, plus
8 hrs marinating**

serves 4

NUTRITIONAL INFORMATION

Calories 243

Protein 39g

Carbohydrate 3g

Sugars 3g

Fat 8g

Saturates 2g

variation

You can also serve this dish with garlic naan bread or plenty of crusty bread, or even freshly cooked rice.

In this adaptation of a traditional Indian recipe for spring chickens, chicken pieces are used, but you could substitute spatchcocked squab chickens (see page 60) if you prefer.

INGREDIENTS

1 tbsp curry paste

1 tbsp tomato ketchup

1 tsp five-spice powder

1 fresh red chile, seeded and
finely chopped

1 tsp Worcestershire sauce

1 tsp sugar

salt

8 skinless chicken pieces

vegetable oil, for brushing

naan bread, to serve

GARNISH

lemon wedges

fresh cilantro sprigs

cook's tip

All curry pastes tend to be quite fiery, but some are hotter than others. Use with caution until you find a variety that suits your palate.

1 Place the curry paste, tomato ketchup, five-spice powder, chile Worcestershire sauce, and sugar in a small bowl, and stir until the sugar has dissolved. Season to taste with salt.

2 Place the chicken pieces in a large, shallow, nonmetallic dish and spoon the spice paste over them, rubbing it in well. Cover with plastic wrap and let marinate in the refrigerator for up to 8 hours.

3 Preheat the barbecue. Remove the chicken from the spice paste, discarding any remaining paste, and brush with oil. Cook the chicken over medium hot coals, turning occasionally, for 25–30 minutes. Briefly heat the naan bread on the barbecue and serve with the chicken, garnished with lemon wedges and cilantro sprigs.

serves 4 **prep: 20 mins, plus 8 hrs marinating** **cook: 10 mins**

This is a delicious dish to serve at a barbecue. Threading the marinated chicken onto the skewers is a messy business, but the results are worth it.

INGREDIENTS

8 tbsp crunchy peanut butter

1 onion, coarsely chopped

1 garlic clove, coarsely chopped

2 tbsp creamed coconut

4 tbsp peanut oil

1 tsp light soy sauce

2 tbsp lime juice

2 fresh red chiles, seeded and chopped

3 kaffir lime leaves, torn

4 skinless, boneless chicken breasts, about 6 oz/175 g each, cut into 1-inch/2.5-cm cubes

---

NUTRITIONAL INFORMATION

Calories 656

Protein 52g

Carbohydrate 8g

Sugars 5g

Fat 47g

Saturates 12g

---

variation

Substitute 1 lb/450 g raw jumbo shrimp for the chicken and cook for 3–4 minutes on each side.

---

cook's tip

Before cooking the chicken skewers on the lit barbecue, brush the grill rack with a little vegetable or corn oil to prevent the meat sticking to it.

1 Put the peanut butter, onion, garlic, coconut, peanut oil, soy sauce, lime juice, chiles, and lime leaves into a food processor and process to a smooth paste. Transfer the paste to a large, glass bowl.

2 Add the chicken cubes to the dish and stir to coat thoroughly. Cover with plastic wrap and let marinate in the refrigerator for up to 8 hours.

3 Preheat the barbecue. Thread the chicken cubes onto several presoaked wooden skewers, reserving the marinade. Cook the skewers over medium hot coals, turning and brushing frequently with the marinade, for 10 minutes, or until thoroughly cooked. Transfer to a large serving plate and serve immediately.

spicy chicken wings

🕐 **cook: 18–20 mins**

🕐 **prep: 15 mins, plus 8 hrs marinating**

serves 4

NUTRITIONAL INFORMATION

Calories 363

Protein 26g

Carbohydrate 29g

Sugars 27g

Fat 16g

Saturates 3g

variation

Substitute the orange and yellow bell peppers for red and green ones. Alternatively, just use red bell peppers.

Coated in a spicy marinade and served with a colorful, chargrilled bell pepper sauce, these delicious chicken wings are perfect as part of a summer barbecue lunch party.

INGREDIENTS

16 chicken wings

4 tbsp corn oil

4 tbsp light soy sauce

2-inch/5-cm piece of fresh gingerroot, coarsely chopped

2 garlic cloves, coarsely chopped

juice and grated rind of 1 lemon

2 tsp ground cinnamon

2 tsp ground turmeric

4 tbsp honey

salt and pepper

SAUCE

2 orange bell peppers

2 yellow bell peppers

corn oil, for brushing

½ cup plain yogurt

2 tbsp dark soy sauce

2 tbsp chopped fresh cilantro

cook's tip

If you prefer, you can snip off the ends of the chicken wings with a pair of strong kitchen scissors to make them look more attractive.

1 Place the chicken wings in a large, shallow, nonmetallic dish. Put the oil, soy sauce, ginger, garlic, lemon rind and juice, cinnamon, turmeric, and honey into a food processor and process to a smooth purée. Season to taste with salt and pepper. Spoon the mixture over the chicken wings and turn until thoroughly coated, cover with plastic wrap and let marinate in the refrigerator for up to 8 hours.

2 Preheat the barbecue. To make the sauce, brush the bell peppers with the oil and cook over hot coals, turning frequently, for 10 minutes, or until the skin is blackened and charred. Remove from the barbecue and let cool slightly, then remove the skins and discard the seeds. Put the flesh into a food processor with the yogurt and process to a smooth purée. Transfer to a bowl and stir in the soy sauce and chopped cilantro.

3 Drain the chicken wings, reserving the marinade. Cook over medium hot coals, turning and brushing frequently with the reserved marinade, for 8–10 minutes, or until thoroughly cooked. Serve immediately with the sauce.

italian deviled chicken

serves 4   **prep: 10 mins, plus 8 hrs marinating**   **cook: 6–10 mins**

Peperoncini, the red chiles of the Abruzzi region of Italy, are so hot that they are known as little devils. They are said to be "as fiery as Lucifer himself."

INGREDIENTS

4 skinless, boneless chicken breasts,
about 6 oz/175 g each, cut into
1-inch/2.5-cm cubes

½ cup olive oil

finely grated rind and juice of 1 lemon

2 garlic cloves, finely chopped

2 tsp finely chopped dried red chiles

salt and pepper

fresh flatleaf parsley sprigs,
to garnish

NUTRITIONAL INFORMATION

Calories 403

Protein 38g

Carbohydrate 1g

Sugars 1g

Fat 28g

Saturates 5g

variation

You can also make these kabobs with dark chicken meat, such as skinless, boneless thighs.

1 Place the chicken cubes in a large, shallow, nonmetallic dish. Place the olive oil, lemon rind and juice, garlic, and chiles in a measuring cup and stir until well blended. Season to taste with salt and pepper.

2 Pour the mixture over the chicken and stir gently to coat. Cover with plastic wrap and let marinate in the refrigerator for up to 8 hours.

3 Preheat the barbecue. Drain the chicken, reserving the marinade. Thread the chicken onto several presoaked wooden skewers and cook over medium hot coals, turning and brushing frequently with the reserved marinade, for 6–10 minutes, or until thoroughly cooked. Transfer to a large serving dish, garnish with parsley sprigs, and serve immediately.

blackened chicken

cook: 6 mins   **prep: 10 mins**   **serves 4**

Blackened dishes—seasoned and chargrilled—are now virtually synonymous with Cajun cooking, but are not, in fact, traditional and were invented relatively recently.

NUTRITIONAL INFORMATION

Calories 229

Protein 39g

Carbohydrate 2g

Sugars 2g

Fat 7g

Saturates 2g

INGREDIENTS

4 skinless, boneless whole chicken breasts, about 6 oz/175 g each

2 tbsp plain yogurt

1 tbsp lemon juice

1 garlic clove, very finely chopped

1 tsp paprika

1 tsp ground cumin

1 tsp mustard powder

½ tsp dried thyme

½ tsp dried oregano

½ tsp cayenne pepper

corn oil, for brushing

thinly sliced onion rings, to garnish

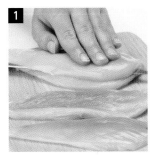

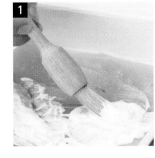

cook's tip

If you like, substitute tuna steaks for the chicken, but don't cut them in half. Cook over medium hot coals for 4 minutes on each side, then serve immediately.

1 Preheat the barbecue. Using a sharp knife, slice the chicken breasts in half horizontally and flatten them slightly with your hand. Place the chicken pieces in a large, shallow, nonmetallic dish. Mix the yogurt and lemon juice together in a small bowl and brush the mixture all over the chicken.

2 Mix the garlic, paprika, cumin, mustard powder, thyme, oregano, and cayenne together in a separate bowl and sprinkle the mixture evenly over the chicken.

3 Brush the chicken pieces with oil and cook over medium hot coals for 3 minutes on each side, or until starting to blacken and the chicken is thoroughly cooked. Transfer to a large serving plate and garnish with thinly sliced onion rings. Serve immediately.

chicken tikka

cook: 15 mins

prep: 15 mins, plus 8 hrs marinating

serves 4

This colorful dish looks immensely appetizing and the aroma as it cooks is out of this world—it lives up to its promise, too.

NUTRITIONAL INFORMATION

Calories 228

Protein 33g

Carbohydrate 9g

Sugars 9g

Fat 7g

Saturates 2g

variation

Add colour to a special occasion dish by using red onions instead of the ordinary yellow onions for the garnish.

INGREDIENTS

1 lb 2 oz/500 g skinless, boneless chicken, cut into 2-inch/5-cm cubes

1 garlic clove, finely chopped

½-inch/1-cm piece fresh gingerroot, finely chopped

⅔ cup plain yogurt

4 tbsp lemon juice

1 tsp chili powder

¼ tsp ground turmeric

1 tbsp chopped fresh cilantro

vegetable oil, for brushing

naan bread, to serve

RAITA

½ cucumber

1 fresh green chile, seeded and finely chopped

1¼ cups plain yogurt

¼ tsp ground cumin

salt

GARNISH

thinly sliced onion rings

fresh cilantro sprigs

lemon wedges

cook's tip

Fresh chiles can burn the skin several hours after chopping, so it is advisable to wear gloves when handling them. Alternatively, wash your hands thoroughly afterwards.

1 Place the chicken in a large glass bowl. Add the garlic, ginger, yogurt, lemon juice, chili powder, turmeric, and cilantro and stir well. Cover with plastic wrap and let marinate in the refrigerator for up to 8 hours.

2 Preheat the barbecue. To make the raita, cut the cucumber into thick slices, then chop finely. Place the cucumber and chile in a bowl and beat in the yogurt with a fork. Stir in the cumin and season to taste with salt. Cover and let chill in the refrigerator until required.

3 Thread the chicken cubes onto presoaked wooden skewers and brush with oil. Cook the chicken over medium hot coals, turning and brushing frequently with oil, for 15 minutes, or until thoroughly cooked. Briefly heat the naan bread on the barbecue. Remove the chicken from the skewers and place on individual serving plates. Garnish with onion rings, cilantro sprigs, and lemon wedges, and serve with the naan bread and the raita.

spicy pita pockets

serves 4 · **prep: 30 mins, plus 2 hrs marinating** · **cook: 35 mins**

For convenience, the chicken is cooked on skewers and then combined with salad to fill pita breads.

INGREDIENTS

1 lb 2 oz/500 g skinless, boneless
chicken, cut into 1-inch/2.5-cm cubes

3 tbsp plain yogurt

1 tsp chili powder

3 tbsp lime juice

1 tbsp chopped fresh cilantro

1 fresh green chile, seeded and
finely chopped

1 tbsp corn oil

salt

4 pita breads

¼ iceberg lettuce, shredded

2 tomatoes, thinly sliced

8 scallions, chopped

1 tbsp lemon juice

8 bottled jalapeño chiles, drained

SAUCE

2 tbsp corn oil

1 onion, chopped

2 garlic cloves, crushed

4 large tomatoes, peeled, seeded,
and chopped

2 fresh red chiles, seeded
and chopped

pinch of ground cumin

salt and pepper

NUTRITIONAL INFORMATION

Calories 519

Protein 39g

Carbohydrate 63g

Sugars 10g

Fat 14g

Saturates 3g

variation

If you prefer a milder dish, omit the
bottled jalapeño chiles and use
1 fresh red chile, seeded and
chopped, added to the sauce.

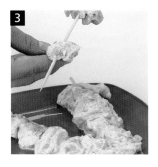

cook's tip

When threading the cubes of
chicken onto the skewers,
leave a small space between
each piece to ensure that the
meat cooks evenly.

1 Place the chicken in
a large bowl. Mix the
yogurt, chili powder, lime juice,
fresh cilantro, green chile,
and corn oil together in a
measuring cup and season
to taste with salt. Pour the
mixture over the chicken
and turn until the chicken is
coated. Cover with plastic
wrap and let marinate in the
refrigerator for 2 hours.

2 Preheat the barbecue.
To make the sauce, heat
the oil in a small pan. Add the
onion and garlic and cook
over low heat, stirring
occasionally, for 10 minutes,
or until softened and golden.
Add the tomatoes, chiles, and
cumin, and season to taste
with salt and pepper. Let
simmer gently for 15 minutes,
or until reduced and thickened.

3 Set the pan of sauce
on the side of the
barbecue to keep warm. Drain
the chicken, reserving the
marinade. Thread the chicken
onto presoaked wooden
skewers. Cook over medium
hot coals, turning and brushing
frequently with the reserved
marinade, for 6–10 minutes,
or until thoroughly cooked.
Meanwhile, slit the pita breads

with a sharp knife and toast
briefly on the barbecue.
Remove the chicken from the
skewers and fill the pita breads
with lettuce, tomato slices,
scallions, and chicken. Sprinkle
with lemon juice and top with
the bottled chiles. Serve
immediately with the sauce.

tarragon turkey

serves 4   **prep: 10 mins** ⏲   **cook: 10–16 mins** ⏲

This economical dish is quick and simple to prepare, and yet it tastes absolutely wonderful, not least because poultry and tarragon have a natural affinity.

INGREDIENTS

4 turkey breasts, about 6 oz/175 g each

salt and pepper

4 tsp whole-grain mustard

8 fresh tarragon sprigs,

plus extra to garnish

4 smoked Canadian bacon strips

salad greens, to serve

NUTRITIONAL INFORMATION	
Calories 296	
Protein 48g	
Carbohydrate 0g	
Sugars 1g	
Fat 11g	
Saturates 4g	

 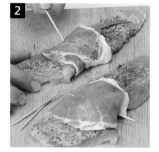

cook's tip

Make sure that you buy genuine French tarragon, as Russian tarragon is coarse and can taste unpleasant. It is not worth using dried tarragon, which has an insipid flavor.

1 Preheat the barbecue. Season the turkey to taste with salt and pepper, and, using a round-bladed knife, spread the mustard evenly over the turkey.

2 Place 2 tarragon sprigs on top of each turkey breast and wrap a bacon strip round it to hold the herbs in place. Secure with a toothpick.

3 Cook the turkey over medium hot coals for 5–8 minutes on each side. Transfer to serving plates and garnish with tarragon sprigs. Serve with salad greens.

turkey rolls

cook: 30 mins　　　　**prep: 20 mins**　　　　**serves 4**

These herb-flavored rolls conceal a soft center of melted cheese as a lovely surprise. They are served here with red currant relish, but would also be delicious with Mild Mustard Sauce (see page 13).

NUTRITIONAL INFORMATION

Calories 430

Protein 54g

Carbohydrate 6g

Sugars 6g

Fat 21g

Saturates 9g

INGREDIENTS

2 tbsp corn oil

salt and pepper

4 tbsp chopped fresh marjoram

4 turkey breast steaks

4 tsp mild mustard

6 oz/175 g Emmental cheese, grated

1 leek, thinly sliced

RELISH

scant ½ cup red currants

2 tbsp chopped fresh mint

2 tsp honey

1 tsp red wine vinegar

cook's tip

You can use fresh or thawed frozen red currants for the relish. To strip fresh red currants from their stalks, run the tines of a fork down the length of the stalk over a bowl.

1 Preheat the barbecue. To make the red currant relish, place all the ingredients in a bowl and mash well with a fork. Season to taste with salt and pepper. Cover with plastic wrap and let chill in the refrigerator until required.

2 Pour the oil into a small bowl, season to taste with pepper, and stir in 2 teaspoons of the marjoram. Set aside. Place the turkey steaks between 2 sheets of plastic wrap and beat with the side of a rolling pin to flatten. Season with salt and pepper and spread the mustard evenly over them. Divide the cheese, leek, and remaining marjoram between the turkey steaks, roll up and tie securely with kitchen string.

3 Brush the turkey rolls with the flavored oil and cook over medium hot coals, turning and brushing frequently with the remaining oil, for 30 minutes. Serve immediately with the red currant relish.

turkey with sun-dried tomato tapenade

⏲ **cook: 10–15 minutes**

⏱ **prep: 10 mins, plus 1 hr marinating**

serves 4

NUTRITIONAL INFORMATION	
Calories	.520
Protein	.44g
Carbohydrate	.4g
Sugars	.2g
Fat	.34g
Saturates	.5g

Sun-dried tomatoes have a marvelously rich, fruity flavor which perfectly complements the marinated turkey—making this dish ideal for a hot summer's day.

INGREDIENTS

4 turkey steaks

MARINADE

⅔ cup white wine
1 tbsp white wine vinegar
1 tbsp olive oil
1 garlic clove, crushed
1 tbsp chopped fresh parsley
pepper

TAPENADE

1 cup sun-dried tomatoes in oil, drained
4 canned anchovy fillets, drained
1 garlic clove, crushed
1 tablespoon lemon juice
3 tablespoons chopped fresh parsley

variation

This dish would also work well with skinless, boneless chicken breasts. Make sure that the chicken is thoroughly cooked before serving.

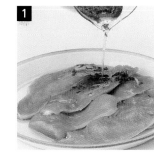

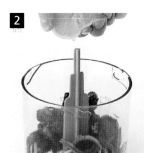

cook's tip

Always marinate the meat in a nonmetallic bowl as the marinade usually contains acidic ingredients, such as vinegar or wine. These may react with a metal bowl and taint the flavor of the meat.

1 Place the turkey steaks in a shallow, nonmetallic dish. Mix all the marinade ingredients together in a measuring cup, whisking well to mix. Pour the marinade over the turkey steaks, turning to coat. Cover with plastic wrap and let marinate in the refrigerator for at least 1 hour.

2 Preheat the barbecue. To make the tapenade, put all the ingredients into a food processor and process to a smooth paste. Transfer to a bowl, cover with plastic wrap, and let chill in the refrigerator until required.

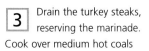

3 Drain the turkey steaks, reserving the marinade. Cook over medium hot coals

for 10–15 minutes, turning and brushing frequently with the reserved marinade. Transfer to 4 large serving plates and top with the sun-dried tomato tapenade. Serve immediately.

turkey with cilantro pesto

serves 4　　　　**prep: 15 mins, plus 2 hrs marinating**　　　　**cook: 10 mins**

Full of Mediterranean flavors, these turkey kabobs would taste fabulous served with a mixed bean salad.

INGREDIENTS

1 lb/450 g skinless, boneless turkey,
cut into 2-inch/5-cm cubes

2 zucchinis, thickly sliced

1 red and 1 yellow bell pepper, seeded
and cut into 2-inch/5-cm squares

8 cherry tomatoes

8 pearl onions

MARINADE

6 tbsp olive oil

3 tbsp dry white wine

1 tsp green peppercorns, crushed

2 tbsp chopped fresh cilantro

salt

CILANTRO PESTO

4 tbsp fresh cilantro leaves

1 tbsp fresh parsley leaves

1 garlic clove

½ cup pine nuts

¼ cup freshly grated
Parmesan cheese

6 tbsp extra virgin olive oil

juice of 1 lemon

NUTRITIONAL INFORMATION

Calories 596

Protein 33g

Carbohydrate 11g

Sugars 8g

Fat 46g

Saturates 7g

variation

Substitute prosciutto for the bacon and for a traditional pesto, replace the cilantro leaves with the same amount of fresh basil leaves.

cook's tip

It is best to use freeze-dried green peppercorns rather than the bottled variety, which tend to taste heavily of vinegar. If you do use bottled ones, drain and rinse before using.

1 Place the turkey in a large glass bowl. To make the marinade, mix the olive oil, wine, peppercorns, and cilantro together in a measuring cup and season to taste with salt. Pour the mixture over the turkey and turn until the turkey is thoroughly coated. Cover with plastic wrap and let marinate in the refrigerator for 2 hours.

2 Preheat the barbecue. To make the pesto, put the cilantro and parsley into a food processor and process until finely chopped. Add the garlic and pine nuts and pulse until chopped. Add the Parmesan cheese, oil, and lemon juice and process briefly to mix. Transfer to a bowl, cover, and let chill in the refrigerator until required.

3 Drain the turkey, reserving the marinade. Thread the turkey, zucchini slices, bell pepper pieces, cherry tomatoes, and onions alternately onto metal skewers. Cook over medium hot coals, turning and brushing frequently with the marinade, for 10 minutes. Serve immediately with the cilantro pesto.

fruity duck

cook: 12–16 mins

prep: 10 minutes

serves 4

NUTRITIONAL INFORMATION

Calories	.368
Protein	.36g
Carbohydrate	.23g
Sugars	.23g
Fat	.15g
Saturates	.5g

variation

Substitute 4 pork chops for the duck and cook over medium hot coals for 8–9 minutes on each side, or until thoroughly cooked.

Apricots and onions counteract the richness of the duck. Its high fat content makes it virtually self-basting, so it stays superbly moist. The duck looks particularly elegant garnished with scallion tassels.

INGREDIENTS

4 duck breasts

⅔ cup no-soak dried apricots

2 shallots, thinly sliced

2 tbsp honey

1 tsp sesame oil

2 tsp Chinese five-spice powder

4 scallions, to garnish

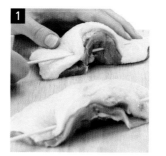

cook's tip

Available from Asian markets, Chinese five-spice powder contains finely ground Sichuan pepper, cassia, fennel seed, star anise, and cloves. It is not the same as Indian five-spice powder.

1 Preheat the barbecue. Using a sharp knife, cut a long slit in the fleshy side of each duck breast to make a pocket. Divide the apricots and shallots between the pockets and secure with skewers.

2 Mix the honey and sesame oil together in a small bowl and brush all over the duck. Sprinkle with the Chinese five-spice powder. To make the garnish, make a few cuts lengthwise down the stem of each scallion. Place in a bowl of ice-cold water and let stand until the tassels open out. Drain well before using.

3 Cook the duck over medium hot coals for 6–8 minutes on each side. Remove the skewers, transfer to a large serving plate, and garnish with the scallion tassels. Serve immediately.

butterflied squab chickens

serves 4　　　**prep: 20 mins, plus 8 hrs marinating**　　　**cook: 25–30 mins**

The squab chickens are coated in a thick mustard paste, which not only gives them a tantalizingly delicious flavor, but also turns them a lovely orange-gold color.

INGREDIENTS

4 squab chickens, about
1 lb/450 g each
1 tbsp paprika
1 tbsp mustard powder
1 tbsp ground cumin
pinch of cayenne pepper

1 tbsp tomato ketchup
1 tbsp lemon juice
salt
5 tbsp melted butter
fresh cilantro sprigs, to garnish

NUTRITIONAL INFORMATION

Calories 583

Protein 40g

Carbohydrate 3g

Sugars 2g

Fat 41g

Saturates 17g

variation

Substitute quail for the squab chickens. Quails are smaller, weighing 4–5 oz/115–140 g, so you will need 8 birds. Cook for 15–20 minutes.

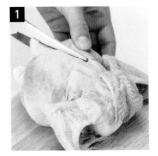

cook's tip

Keep a close watch on the squab chickens while cooking and if they look as if they are drying out, brush with a little corn oil.

1 To spatchcock the squab chicken, turn 1 bird breast-side down and, using strong kitchen scissors or poultry shears, cut through the skin and rib cage along both sides of the backbone, from tail to neck. Remove the backbone and turn the bird breast-side up. Press down firmly on the breastbone to flatten. Fold the wingtips

underneath. Push a skewer through one wing, the top of the breast, and out of the other wing. Push a second skewer through one thigh, the bottom of the breast, and out through the other thigh. Repeat with the remaining squab chickens.

2 Mix the paprika, mustard powder, cumin,

cayenne, tomato ketchup, and lemon juice together in a small bowl and season to taste with salt. Gradually stir in the butter to make a smooth paste. Spread the paste evenly over the squab chickens, cover, and let marinate in the refrigerator for up to 8 hours.

3 Preheat the barbecue. Cook the squab

chickens over medium hot coals, turning frequently, for 25–30 minutes, brushing with a little oil if necessary. Transfer to a serving plate, garnish with fresh cilantro sprigs and serve.

chicken livers with sweet-&-sour relish

cook: 10 mins **prep: 15 mins** serves 4

NUTRITIONAL INFORMATION

Calories	.315
Protein	.24g
Carbohydrate	.28g
Sugars	.27g
Fat	.13g
Saturates	.4g

variation

Other vegetables would also work well, such as small strips of red or orange bell pepper and zucchini sticks instead of the white mushrooms.

Both liver and bacon and prunes and bacon are well-known combinations, and here they are mixed with cherry tomatoes and mushrooms and served with a savory relish for a taste sensation.

INGREDIENTS

12 oz/350 g chicken livers

4 oz/115 g lean bacon
strips, rinded

8 no-soak dried prunes

8 cherry tomatoes

8 white mushrooms

corn oil, for brushing

SWEET-&-SOUR RELISH

5 tbsp sweet pickle

3 tbsp tomato ketchup

3 tbsp brown sauce

4½ tsp cider vinegar

4½ tsp Worcestershire sauce

cook's tip

Dried no-soak fruit is the same as the dried, but moist, ready-to-eat fruit. It is available in health foodstores and most large food stores.

1 Preheat the barbecue. To make the relish, place all the ingredients in a bowl and mix together. Cover with plastic wrap and set aside until required.

2 Rinse the chicken livers in cold water and pat dry with paper towels. Cut the bacon strips in half. Wrap a piece of bacon round each chicken liver and secure with a toothpick. Wrap a prune round the base of each tomato. Thread the chicken livers, prune-wrapped tomatoes, and mushrooms onto presoaked wooden skewers and brush with oil.

3 Cook over medium hot coals for 5 minutes on each side. Remove the skewers, transfer to a large serving plate, and serve immediately with the relish.

meat

For many people, barbecues mean plenty of meat and this chapter will not disappoint them. Steaks, chops, ribs, kabobs, sausages, and burgers appear in many guises, from fragrant lamb in Rack & Ruin (see page 102) to bacon-wrapped sausages in Pigs in Blankets (see page 121). Popular barbecue favorites include Beef Satay (see page 97), Shashlik (see page 110), and Chinese Ribs (see page 115), while more unusual dishes range from Sozzled Lamb Chops (see page 112) to Meatballs on Sticks (see page 118). Those with a hearty appetite might like to tackle Easy Mixed Grill (see page 122), while anyone who has ever been disappointed by ready-made hamburgers—and who hasn't?— will love Best-Ever Burgers (see page 90).

Marinades are a very important aspect of preparing meat for the barbecue, as they often help to tenderize it to a melt-in-the-mouth texture. Ideally, prepare the ingredients the night before the barbecue and let the meat marinate overnight in the refrigerator. This also allows the flavors to mingle and permeate the meat. Recipes range from hot and spicy to cool and minty, and from sophisticated and subtle to robust and hearty.

As with the poultry recipes, you can mix and match the sauces or use one from the beginning of the book. Try serving Tabasco Steaks (see page 92) with Guacamole (see page 13) instead of Watercress Butter for example, or Tomato Relish (see page 94) with Spicy Lamb Steaks (see page 104). Experiment and enjoy.

best-ever burgers

⏲ **cook: 6–8 mins**   ⏱ **prep: 10 mins**   **serves 6**

Barbecues and burgers are almost inseparable. However, these succulent, homemade burgers bear no resemblance to the little ready-made patties available in most stores.

NUTRITIONAL INFORMATION

Calories	.659
Protein	.44g
Carbohydrate	.66g
Sugars	.8g
Fat	.26g
Saturates	.5g

variation

For Tex-Mex burgers, add 2 seeded and finely chopped fresh green chiles to the mixture in Step 1 and serve with Guacamole (see page 13).

INGREDIENTS

4 cups lean ground steak

2 onions, finely chopped

½ cup fresh white bread crumbs

1 egg, lightly beaten

1½ teaspoons finely chopped fresh thyme

salt and pepper

TO SERVE

6 sesame seed baps

2 tomatoes

1 onion

lettuce leaves

Mayonnaise (see page 13)

mustard

tomato ketchup

cook's tip

Homemade burgers have a much looser texture than ready-made ones, so use a spatula to turn them carefully and remove from the barbecue as soon as they are cooked.

1 Preheat the barbecue. Place the steak, onions, bread crumbs, egg, and thyme in a large glass bowl and season to taste with salt and pepper. Mix thoroughly using your hands.

2 Form the mixture into 6 large patties with your hands and a round-bladed knife.

3 Cook the burgers over hot coals for 3–4 minutes on each side. Meanwhile, cut the baps in half and briefly toast on the barbecue, cut-side down. Using a sharp knife, slice the tomatoes and cut the onion into thinly sliced rings. Fill the toasted baps with the cooked burgers, lettuce, sliced tomatoes, and onion rings, and serve immediately, with the Mayonnaise, mustard, and tomato ketchup.

tabasco steaks with watercress butter

serves 4   **prep: 10 mins**   **cook: 5–12 mins**

A variation on a classic theme, this simple, but rather extravagant dish would be ideal for a special occasion barbecue party.

INGREDIENTS

1 bunch of watercress

3 oz/85 g unsalted butter, softened

4 sirloin steaks, about 8 oz/225 g each

4 tsp Tabasco sauce

salt and pepper

NUTRITIONAL INFORMATION

Calories 462

Protein 53g

Carbohydrate 0g

Sugars 0g

Fat 28g

Saturates 16g

variation

If you like, substitute the same amount of fresh parsley for the watercress. Alternatively, serve the steaks with Cilantro Pesto (see page 80).

1 Preheat the barbecue. Using a sharp knife, finely chop enough watercress to fill 4 tablespoons. Set aside a few watercress leaves for the garnish. Place the butter in a small bowl and beat in the chopped watercress with a fork until fully incorporated. Cover with plastic wrap and let chill in the refrigerator until required.

2 Sprinkle each steak with 1 teaspoon of the Tabasco sauce, rubbing it in well. Season to taste with salt and pepper.

3 Cook the steaks over hot coals for 2½ minutes each side for rare, 4 minutes each side for medium, and 6 minutes each side for well done. Transfer to serving plates, garnish with the reserved watercress leaves, and serve immediately, topped with the watercress butter.

steak packages

cook: 10 mins   **prep: 10 mins, plus 8 hrs marinating**   serves 4

A red wine marinade is perfect for steak, as it imparts a delicious flavor and tenderizes the meat to a melt-in-the-mouth consistency.

NUTRITIONAL INFORMATION	
Calories	.466
Protein	.54g
Carbohydrate	.3g
Sugars	.2g
Fat	.21g
Saturates	.9g

INGREDIENTS

4 sirloin or rump steaks

1¼ cups dry red wine

2 tbsp olive oil

salt and pepper

1 oz/25 g butter

2 tsp Dijon mustard

4 shallots, finely chopped

4 fresh thyme sprigs

4 bay leaves

variation

If you like, substitute the same amount of creamed horseradish for the mustard and use fresh marjoram sprigs instead of the thyme.

1 Place the steaks in a large, shallow, nonmetallic dish. Mix the wine and oil together in a measuring cup and season to taste with salt and pepper. Pour the marinade over the steaks, cover with plastic wrap, and let marinate in the refrigerator for up to 8 hours.

2 Preheat the barbecue. Cut out 4 squares of foil large enough to enclose the steaks and coat the centers with the butter and mustard. Drain the steaks and place them on the foil squares. Top with the shallots, thyme, and bay leaves and fold over the foil to make neat packages.

3 Cook the packages over hot coals for 10 minutes, turning once. Serve the steaks immediately in the packages.

mustard steaks with tomato relish

serves 4　　　　　　**prep: 10 mins, plus** ⏲
1 hr cooling/standing　　　　　　**cook: 50–60 mins** ⏲

Tarragon mustard gives these steaks a subtle spicy flavor that contrasts well with the sharp taste of the sweet-and-sour tomato relish. Serve with a salad and potatoes for a filling main course.

INGREDIENTS

4 sirloin or rump steaks

1 tbsp tarragon mustard

2 garlic cloves, crushed

fresh tarragon sprigs, to garnish

TOMATO RELISH

2 cups cherry tomatoes

2 tbsp brown sugar

¼ cup white wine vinegar

1 piece of preserved ginger, chopped

½ lime, thinly sliced

salt

NUTRITIONAL INFORMATION

Calories 380

Protein 54g

Carbohydrate 18g

Sugars 17g

Fat 11g

Saturates 5g

variation

Substitute a differently flavored mustard—there is a huge variety available these days, including chili, whiskey, and Champagne flavor.

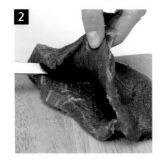

cook's tip

Use long-handled tongs to turn the steaks over. Try to avoid using a fork as this will pierce the meat and some of the delicious juices will be lost.

1 To make the tomato relish, place all the ingredients in a heavy-bottom pan, seasoning to taste with salt. Bring to a boil, stirring until the sugar has completely dissolved. Reduce the heat and let simmer, stirring occasionally, for 40 minutes, or until thickened. Transfer to a bowl, cover with plastic wrap and let cool.

2 Preheat the barbecue. Using a sharp knife, cut almost completely through each steak horizontally to make a pocket. Spread the mustard inside the pockets and rub the steaks all over with the garlic. Place them on a plate, cover with plastic wrap and let stand for 30 minutes.

3 Cook the steaks over hot coals for 2½ minutes each side for rare, 4 minutes each side for medium, or 6 minutes each side for well done. Transfer to serving plates, garnish with fresh tarragon sprigs, and serve immediately with the tomato relish.

luxury cheeseburgers

serves 4 | **prep: 15 mins** | **cook: 10 mins**

This is a sophisticated version of the traditional burger with a surprise filling of melted blue cheese. Serve with plenty of salad leaves to make a substantial barbecue lunch.

INGREDIENTS

2 oz/55 g Stilton cheese

2 cups lean ground steak

1 onion, finely chopped

1 celery stalk, finely chopped

1 tsp creamed horseradish

1 tbsp chopped fresh thyme

salt and pepper

TO SERVE

4 sesame seed baps

lettuce leaves

sliced tomatoes

NUTRITIONAL INFORMATION	
Calories	.360
Protein	.32g
Carbohydrate	.32g
Sugars	.4g
Fat	.13g
Saturates	.5g

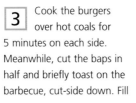

variation

Substitute Lancashire or another semifirm cheese for the Stilton and snipped chives for the thyme.

1 Preheat the barbecue. Crumble the Stilton into a bowl and set aside until required. Place the steak, onion, celery, horseradish, and thyme in a separate bowl and season to taste with salt and pepper. Mix well using your hands.

2 Form the mixture into 8 patties with your hands and a round-bladed knife. Divide the cheese between 4 of them and top with the remaining patties. Gently press them together and mold the edges.

3 Cook the burgers over hot coals for 5 minutes on each side. Meanwhile, cut the baps in half and briefly toast on the barbecue, cut-side down. Fill the baps with the cooked burgers, lettuce, and tomato slices, and serve immediately.

beef satay

cook: 5–8 mins

prep: 10 mins, plus 2 hrs marinating

serves 6

Many Westerners assume that a satay must involve a peanut sauce, but this is not always true. The term simply refers to a kabob that has been marinated in a flavorsome mixture of any kind.

NUTRITIONAL INFORMATION

Calories	.258
Protein	.37g
Carbohydrate	.4g
Sugars	.3g
Fat	.11g
Saturates	.4g

INGREDIENTS

2 lb 4 oz/1 kg rump steak

1 tbsp honey

2 tbsp dark soy sauce

2 tbsp peanut oil

1 garlic clove, finely chopped

1 tsp ground coriander

1 tsp caraway seeds

pinch of chili powder

lime wedges, to garnish

cook's tip

Instead of cutting the steak into small cubes, slice it into long narrow strips, and thread the strips in zigzags onto the skewers.

1 Using a sharp knife, cut the steak into 1-inch/2.5-cm cubes, then place in a large, shallow, nonmetallic dish. Mix the honey, soy sauce, oil, garlic, coriander, caraway seeds, and chili powder together in a small measuring cup. Pour the mixture over the steak and stir until the steak is thoroughly coated with the marinade. Cover with plastic wrap and let marinate in the refrigerator for 2 hours, turning occasionally.

2 Preheat the barbecue. Drain the steak, reserving the marinade. Thread the steak onto several presoaked wooden skewers.

3 Cook the steak over hot coals, turning and brushing frequently with the reserved marinade, for 5–8 minutes. Transfer to a large serving plate, garnish with lime wedges, and serve.

beef, lamb & bacon brochettes

serves 4　　　　**prep: 15 mins** ⏱　　　　**cook: 15–20 mins** ♨

This is a veritable feast for meat-lovers—satisfying, easy to prepare skewers, served with a rich tomato sauce.

INGREDIENTS

14 oz/400 g rump steak, cut into
1-inch/2.5-cm cubes

14 oz/400 g boneless leg of lamb, cut
into 1-inch/2.5-cm cubes

8 Canadian bacon strips, rinded and
cut into thin strips

8 shallots, halved

8 tomatoes, halved

12 bottled chiles, drained

4 tbsp corn oil

4 garlic cloves, finely chopped

2 tsp paprika

¼ tsp cayenne pepper

TOMATO SAUCE

8 oz/225 g tomatoes, peeled
and chopped

1 onion, finely chopped

1 green bell pepper, seeded and
finely chopped

3 tbsp finely chopped fresh parsley

3 tbsp tomato ketchup

pinch of sugar

pinch of chili powder

salt and pepper

NUTRITIONAL INFORMATION

Calories 675

Protein 59g

Carbohydrate 18g

Sugars 15g

Fat 42g

Saturates 14g

variation

Other vegetables would be suitable to use as part of the kabobs, such as onion wedges and small strips of red or yellow bell pepper.

cook's tip

Make sure that the skewers you use are long enough and try not to overcrowd them on the barbecue rack, otherwise the food will not cook evenly. If space is a problem, cook the brochettes in batches.

1 Preheat the barbecue. To make the tomato sauce, rub the tomatoes through a fine strainer into a small bowl, then stir in the onion, green bell pepper, parsley, tomato ketchup, and sugar, and season to taste with chili powder, salt and pepper. Cover with plastic wrap and let chill in the refrigerator until required.

2 Thread the steak, lamb, bacon, shallots, tomatoes, and chiles alternately onto 4 metal or presoaked wooden skewers. Mix the oil, garlic, paprika, and cayenne together in a small bowl. Brush the brochettes with the oil.

3 Cook the brochettes over medium hot coals, turning and brushing frequently with the spicy oil, for 15–20 minutes. Transfer to a large serving plate and serve immediately with the tomato sauce.

indonesian beef kabobs

cook: 10 mins

**prep: 15 mins, plus
2 hrs marinating/standing**

serves 4

NUTRITIONAL INFORMATION

Calories 175

Protein 26g

Carbohydrate 8g

Sugars 6g

Fat 5g

Saturates 2g

*These spicy Indonesian kabobs are traditionally served with
sambal kecap—a delicious chili-flavored dipping sauce—and
a refreshing cucumber salad.*

INGREDIENTS

1 tsp coriander seeds

½ tsp cumin seeds

1 lb/450 g rump steak cut into strips

1 onion

2 garlic cloves

1 tbsp brown sugar

1 tbsp dark soy sauce

4 tbsp lemon juice

salt

SAUCE

1 fresh red chile

4 tbsp dark soy sauce

2 garlic cloves, finely chopped

4 tsp lemon juice

2 tbsp hot water

variation

Add extra hotness to the sauce by
using 1–2 very hot fresh Thai chiles.
Remember to wash your hands
thoroughly after chopping.

cook's tip

If you don't have a mortar and
pestle handy, then you can
grind the coriander and cumin
seeds in a spice mill or even a
clean coffee grinder.

1 To make the sauce,
using a sharp knife,
deseed the chile and finely
chop. Place in a small bowl
with all the other sauce
ingredients and mix together.
Cover with plastic wrap and let
stand until required.

2 Dry-fry the coriander
and cumin seeds in a
skillet for 1 minute, or until
they give off their aroma and
start to pop. Remove from the
heat and grind in a mortar
with a pestle. Place the steak
in a shallow, nonmetallic dish
and add the ground spices,
stirring to coat. Put the onion,
garlic, sugar, soy sauce, and
lemon juice into a food
processor and process to a
paste. Season to taste with salt
and spoon the mixture over
the steak, turning to coat.
Cover with plastic wrap and let
marinate in the refrigerator for
2 hours.

3 Preheat the barbecue.
Drain the steak,
reserving the marinade, and
thread it onto several
presoaked wooden or metal
skewers. Cook over hot coals,
turning and basting frequently
with the reserved marinade, for
5–8 minutes, until thoroughly
cooked. Transfer to a large
serving plate and serve with
the sauce for dipping.

serves 4　　　　　**prep: 10 mins, plus 1 hr marinating**　　　　　**cook: 20 mins**

This quick and easy dish is perfect for serving as part of a summer party menu, along with plenty of salad and potatoes.

INGREDIENTS

4 racks of lamb, each with 4 chops

2 tbsp extra virgin olive oil

1 tbsp balsamic vinegar

1 tbsp lemon juice

3 tbsp finely chopped fresh rosemary

1 small onion, finely chopped

salt and pepper

NUTRITIONAL INFORMATION

Calories 798

Protein 46g

Carbohydrate 2g

Sugars 1g

Fat 68g

Saturates 31g

cook's tip

Balsamic vinegar is a smooth, mellow-flavored dark vinegar made in the region surrounding Modena in northern Italy. It is quite expensive, but has a unique flavor.

1 Place the racks of lamb in a large, shallow, nonmetallic dish. Place the oil, vinegar, lemon juice, rosemary, and onion in a measuring cup and stir together. Season to taste with salt and pepper.

2 Pour the marinade over the lamb and turn until thoroughly coated. Cover with plastic wrap and let marinate in the refrigerator for 1 hour, turning occasionally.

3 Preheat the barbecue. Drain the racks of lamb, reserving the marinade. Cook over medium hot coals, brushing frequently with the marinade, for 10 minutes on each side. Serve immediately.

soy pork with coriander

cook: 14–20 mins

prep: 10 mins, plus 1 hr marinating

serves 4

The spicy, Eastern-style flavors that suffuse these pork chops will make them an unusual and original barbecue favorite.

NUTRITIONAL INFORMATION

Calories 469

Protein 40g

Carbohydrate 3g

Sugars 1g

Fat 33g

Saturates 12g

INGREDIENTS

4 pork chops, about 6 oz/175 g each

1 tbsp coriander seeds

6 black peppercorns

4 tbsp dark soy sauce

1 garlic clove, finely chopped

1 tsp sugar

fresh cilantro sprigs, to garnish

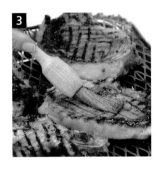

cook's tip

It is worth taking the time to find a good-quality soy sauce for the aromatic marinade that flavors these chops. Asian markets stock the best range of sauces.

1 Place the pork chops in a large, shallow, nonmetallic dish. Crush the coriander seeds and peppercorns in a spice mill. Alternatively, place in a mortar and crush with a pestle. Place the soy sauce, garlic, sugar, crushed coriander seeds, and peppercorns in a measuring cup and stir well until the sugar has dissolved.

2 Pour the soy sauce mixture over the chops, turning to coat. Cover with plastic wrap and let marinate in the refrigerator for 1 hour, turning occasionally.

3 Preheat the barbecue. Drain the chops, reserving the marinade. Cook over medium hot coals, brushing frequently with the reserved marinade, for 7–10 minutes on each side. Transfer to a large serving plate, garnish with fresh cilantro sprigs, and serve.

spicy lamb steaks

cook: 40 mins

prep: 15 mins, plus 3 hrs 20 mins cooling/marinating   serves 4

Lamb, fresh rosemary, and bay leaves always go so well together, and in this delicious dish a hot and spicy marinade is used to give the lamb an extra special flavor.

NUTRITIONAL INFORMATION	
Calories	.490
Protein	.39g
Carbohydrate	.23g
Sugars	.20g
Fat	.28g
Saturates	.9g

variation

Many different marinades will work equally well for this lamb dish. Try a White Wine Marinade or a Hot Pepper Marinade (see page 13).

INGREDIENTS

4 lamb steaks, about 6 oz/175 g each

8 fresh rosemary sprigs

8 fresh bay leaves

2 tbsp olive oil

SPICY MARINADE

2 tbsp corn oil

1 large onion, finely chopped

2 garlic cloves, finely chopped

2 tbsp Jamaican jerk seasoning

1 tbsp curry paste

1 tsp grated fresh gingerroot

14 oz/400 g canned chopped tomatoes

4 tbsp Worcestershire sauce

3 tbsp light brown sugar

salt and pepper

cook's tip

You can buy ready-made Jamaican jerk seasoning at most supermarkets. Alternatively, make your own, following Step 1 of the recipe for Jerk Chicken on page 61.

1 To make the marinade, heat the oil in a heavy-bottom pan. Add the onion and garlic and cook, stirring occasionally, for 5 minutes, or until softened. Stir in the jerk seasoning, curry paste, and grated ginger, and cook, stirring constantly, for 2 minutes. Add the tomatoes, Worcestershire sauce, and sugar, then season to taste

with salt and pepper. Bring to a boil, stirring constantly, then reduce the heat and let simmer for 15 minutes, or until thickened. Remove from the heat and let cool.

2 Place the lamb steaks between 2 sheets of plastic wrap and beat with the side of a rolling pin to flatten. Transfer the steaks to a large,

shallow, nonmetallic dish. Pour the marinade over them, turning to coat. Cover with plastic wrap and let marinate in the refrigerator for 3 hours.

3 Preheat the barbecue. Drain the lamb, reserving the marinade. Cook the lamb over medium hot coals, brushing frequently with the marinade, for 5–7 minutes

on each side. Meanwhile, dip the rosemary and bay leaves in the olive oil and cook on the barbecue for 3–5 minutes. Serve the lamb immediately with the herbs.

minted lamb chops

serves 6　　　　**prep: 15 mins, plus 2 hrs marinating** ⏲　　　　**cook: 10–14 mins** 🔥

You can prepare this dish with any kind of lamb chops, such as loin chops or leg chops, which are especially tender. Shoulder steaks also work well in this recipe.

INGREDIENTS

6 chump chops, about 6 oz/175 g each

⅔ cup strained plain yogurt

2 garlic cloves, finely chopped

1 tsp grated fresh gingerroot

¼ tsp coriander seeds, crushed

salt and pepper

1 tbsp olive oil, plus extra for brushing

1 tbsp orange juice

1 tsp walnut oil

2 tbsp chopped fresh mint

NUTRITIONAL INFORMATION	
Calories	.420
Protein	.30g
Carbohydrate	.1g
Sugars	.1g
Fat	.33g
Saturates	.15g

variation

If you like, omit the orange juice and walnut oil and stir in ¼ teaspoon ground star anise and a pinch each of ground cinnamon and ground cumin.

1 Place the chops in a large, shallow, nonmetallic bowl. Mix half the yogurt, the garlic, ginger, and coriander seeds together in a measuring cup and season to taste with salt and pepper. Spoon the mixture over the chops, turning to coat, then cover with plastic wrap and let marinate in the refrigerator for 2 hours, turning occasionally.

2 Preheat the barbecue. Place the remaining yogurt, the olive oil, orange juice, walnut oil, and mint in a small bowl and, using a hand-held whisk, whisk until thoroughly blended. Season to taste with salt and pepper. Cover the minted yogurt with plastic wrap and let chill in the refrigerator until ready to serve.

3 Drain the chops, scraping off the marinade. Brush with olive oil and cook over medium hot coals for 5–7 minutes on each side. Serve immediately with the minted yogurt.

normandy brochettes

cook: 12–15 mins

prep: 10 mins, plus 1–2 hrs marinating

serves 4

The orchards of Normandy are famous throughout France, providing both eating apples and cider-making varieties. For an authentic touch, enjoy a glass of Calvados between courses.

NUTRITIONAL INFORMATION	
Calories	242
Protein	24g
Carbohydrate	8g
Sugars	8g
Fat	11g
Saturates	3g

INGREDIENTS

1 lb/450 g pork fillet

1¼ cups hard cider

1 tbsp finely chopped fresh sage

6 black peppercorns, crushed

2 crisp eating apples

1 tbsp corn oil

variation

Replace 1 apple with 6 no-soak dried prunes wrapped in strips of lean bacon. Thread the prunes onto the skewers with the remaining apple and pork.

1 Using a sharp knife, cut the pork into 1-inch/2.5-cm cubes, then place in a large, shallow, nonmetallic dish. Mix the cider, sage, and peppercorns together in a measuring cup, pour the mixture over the pork and turn until thoroughly coated. Cover and let marinate in the refrigerator for 1–2 hours.

2 Preheat the barbecue. Drain the pork, reserving the marinade. Core the apples, but do not peel, then cut into wedges. Dip the apple wedges into the reserved marinade and thread onto several metal skewers, alternating with the cubes of pork. Stir the corn oil into the remaining marinade.

3 Cook the brochettes over medium hot coals, turning and brushing frequently with the reserved marinade, for 12–15 minutes. Transfer to a large serving plate and if you prefer, remove the meat and apples from the skewers before serving. Serve immediately.

serves 4

prep: 20 mins, plus 2 hrs marinating

cook: 10–15 mins

Turkey, the bridge between East and West, has an eclectic mix of influences in its cooking style. These traditional kabobs would originally have been made with mutton or, possibly, young goat.

INGREDIENTS

1 lb 2 oz/500 g boned shoulder of lamb, cut into 1-inch/2.5-cm cubes

1 tbsp olive oil

2 tbsp dry white wine

2 tbsp finely chopped fresh mint

4 garlic cloves, finely chopped

2 tsp grated orange rind

1 tbsp paprika

1 tsp sugar

salt and pepper

SESAME SEED CREAM

8 oz/225 g sesame seed paste

2 garlic cloves, finely chopped

2 tbsp extra virgin olive oil

2 tbsp lemon juice

½ cup water

NUTRITIONAL INFORMATION

Calories 752

Protein 43g

Carbohydrate 2g

Sugars 1g

Fat 63g

Saturates 16g

variation

You can also serve these kabobs with other sauces, such as Tsatziki (see page 153) or even a Tomato Sauce (see page 98).

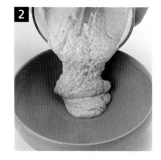

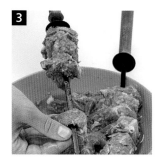

cook's tip

Sesame seed paste or tahini is available from most supermarkets and specialist foodstores. It is made from ground, pulped sesame seeds.

1 Place the lamb cubes in a large, shallow, nonmetallic dish. Mix the olive oil, wine, mint, garlic, orange rind, paprika, and sugar together in a measuring cup and season to taste with salt and pepper. Pour the mixture over the lamb, turning to coat, then cover and let marinate in the refrigerator for 2 hours, turning occasionally.

2 Preheat the barbecue. To make the sesame seed cream, put the sesame seed paste, garlic, oil, and lemon juice into a food processor and process briefly to mix. With the motor still running, gradually add the water through the feeder tube until smooth. Transfer to a bowl, cover, and let chill in the refrigerator until required.

3 Drain the lamb, reserving the marinade, and thread it onto several long metal skewers. Cook over medium hot coals, turning and brushing frequently with the reserved marinade, for 10–15 minutes. Serve with the sesame seed cream.

shashlik

cook: 10–15 mins

prep: 20 mins, plus 8 hrs marinating

serves 4

Fragrant, lemon–flavored kabobs, shashlik are a Georgian speciality from the fertile area between the Black Sea and the Caucasian Mountains in the Russian Federation. They have much in common with neighboring Turkey's shish kabobs.

NUTRITIONAL INFORMATION	
Calories	486
Protein	42g
Carbohydrate	5g
Sugars	4g
Fat	34g
Saturates	11g

INGREDIENTS

1 lb 8 oz/675 g boneless leg of lamb, cut into 1-inch/2.5-cm cubes

12 large mushrooms

4 lean bacon strips, rinded

8 cherry tomatoes

1 large green bell pepper, seeded and cut into squares

fresh herb sprigs, to garnish

MARINADE

4 tbsp corn oil

4 tbsp lemon juice

1 onion, finely chopped

½ tsp dried rosemary

½ tsp dried thyme

salt and pepper

variation

If you like, you can use other marinades to flavor the lamb, such as White Wine Marinade (see page 13).

cook's tip

When barbecuing all types of kabobs, make sure that they are brushed with the marinade or oil and turned frequently, otherwise they may burn.

1 Place the lamb and mushrooms in a large, shallow, nonmetallic dish. Mix all the ingredients for the marinade together in a measuring cup, seasoning to taste with salt and pepper. Pour the mixture over the lamb and mushrooms, turning to coat. Cover with plastic wrap and let marinate in the refrigerator for up to 8 hours.

2 Preheat the barbecue. Cut the bacon strips in half across the center and stretch with a heavy, flat-bladed knife, then roll up. Drain the lamb and mushrooms, reserving the marinade. Thread the bacon rolls, lamb, mushrooms, tomatoes, and bell pepper squares alternately onto metal skewers. Strain the marinade.

3 Cook the kabobs over medium hot coals, turning and brushing frequently with the reserved marinade, for 10–15 minutes. Transfer to a large serving plate, garnish with fresh herb sprigs, and serve immediately.

sozzled lamb chops

serves 4 **prep: 15 mins, plus 5 mins marinating** **cook: 10 mins**

These chops will only need marinating for a short time, as the marinade is quite strongly flavored. They are delicious served with a rich, tasty mustard butter.

INGREDIENTS

8 lamb loin chops

fresh parsley sprigs, to garnish

salad, to serve

2 tbsp lemon juice

2 tbsp dry gin

1 garlic clove, finely chopped

salt and pepper

MARINADE

2 tbsp extra virgin olive oil

2 tbsp Worcestershire sauce

MUSTARD BUTTER

2 oz/55 g unsalted butter, softened

1½ tsp tarragon mustard

1 tbsp chopped fresh parsley

dash of lemon juice

NUTRITIONAL INFORMATION

Calories 770

Protein 52g

Carbohydrate 2g

Sugars 1g

Fat 60g

Saturates 29g

variation

Instead of mustard butter, serve the chops with Watercress Butter (see page 92) and garnish with fresh watercress instead of parsley.

cook's tip

Make sure that the barbecue has reached the correct temperature before cooking, otherwise you will only blacken the food on the outside and the inside will still be raw.

1 Preheat the barbecue. Place the lamb chops in a large, shallow, nonmetallic dish. Mix all the ingredients for the marinade together in a measuring cup, seasoning to taste with salt and pepper. Pour the mixture over the chops and then turn them until they are well coated. Cover with plastic wrap and let marinate for 5 minutes.

2 To make the mustard butter, mix all the ingredients together in a small bowl, beating with a fork until well blended. Cover with plastic wrap and let chill in the refrigerator until required.

3 Drain the chops, reserving the marinade. Cook over medium hot coals, brushing frequently with the reserved marinade, for 5 minutes on each side. Transfer to serving plates, top with the mustard butter, and garnish with parsley sprigs. Serve immediately with salad.

hot & spicy ribs

serves 4 **prep: 15 mins** **cook: 1 hr**

Twice-cooked (first in the kitchen and then on the barbecue), these succulent, pork spareribs are deliciously tender and packed full of spicy flavors.

INGREDIENTS

1 onion, chopped

2 garlic cloves, chopped

1-inch/2.5-cm piece fresh
gingerroot, sliced

1 fresh red chile, seeded
and chopped

5 tbsp dark soy sauce

3 tbsp lime juice

1 tbsp jaggery or brown sugar

2 tbsp peanut oil

salt and pepper

2 lb 4 oz/1 kg pork spareribs, separated

NUTRITIONAL INFORMATION

Calories	.466
Protein	.38g
Carbohydrate	.11g
Sugars	.7g
Fat	.30g
Saturates	.10g

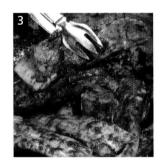

cook's tip

Peanut oil is used extensively in South-east Asian cooking. It is usually available in most large supermarkets, but if you cannot find it, then use sunflower-seed oil instead.

1 Preheat the barbecue. Put the onion, garlic, ginger, chile, and soy sauce into a food processor and process to a paste. Transfer to a measuring cup and stir in the lime juice, sugar, and oil. Season with salt and pepper.

2 Place the spareribs in a preheated wok or large,

heavy-bottom pan and pour in the soy sauce mixture. Place on the stove and bring to a boil, then let simmer over low heat, stirring frequently, for 30 minutes. If the mixture appears to be drying out, add a little water.

3 Remove the spareribs, reserving the sauce.

Cook the ribs over medium hot coals, turning and basting frequently with the sauce, for 20–30 minutes. Transfer to a large serving plate and serve immediately.

chinese ribs

cook: 30–40 mins   **prep: 10 mins, plus 6 hrs marinating**   **serves 4**

Leave these pork spareribs to marinate for as long as possible to ensure that the wonderful flavors of the marinade mingle and thoroughly permeate the meat.

NUTRITIONAL INFORMATION	
Calories	.450
Protein	.38g
Carbohydrate	.14g
Sugars	.12g
Fat	.27g
Saturates	.9g

INGREDIENTS

2 lb 4 oz/1 kg pork spareribs, separated

4 tbsp dark soy sauce

3 tbsp brown sugar

1 tbsp peanut or sunflower-seed oil

2 garlic cloves, finely chopped

2 tsp Chinese five-spice powder

½-inch/1-cm piece fresh gingerroot, grated

shredded scallions, to garnish

variation

Marinate the meat in 4 tablespoons each soy sauce and honey, 1 tablespoon water, 1 teaspoon mustard powder, and a pinch of cayenne pepper.

1 Place the spareribs in a large, shallow, nonmetallic dish. Mix the soy sauce, sugar, oil, garlic, Chinese five-spice powder, and ginger together in a measuring cup. Pour the mixture over the ribs and turn until the ribs are well coated in the marinade.

2 Cover the dish with plastic wrap and let marinate in the refrigerator for at least 6 hours.

3 Preheat the barbecue. Drain the ribs, reserving the marinade. Cook over medium hot coals, turning and brushing frequently with the reserved marinade, for 30–40 minutes. Transfer to a large serving dish, garnish with the shredded scallions, and serve immediately.

lemon & herb pork scallops

serves 4   **prep: 10 mins, plus 8 hrs**
30 mins cooling/marinating   **cook: 15 mins**

Although it is always important that pork is well done, be careful not to overcook these delicately flavored, thin scallops and be sure to grill them only on a medium barbecue.

INGREDIENTS

4 pork scallops

2 tbsp corn oil

6 bay leaves, torn into pieces

grated rind and juice of 2 lemons

½ cup beer

1 tbsp honey

6 juniper berries, lightly crushed

salt and pepper

1 crisp eating apple

fresh flatleaf parsley sprigs,
to garnish

NUTRITIONAL INFORMATION	
Calories	349
Protein	37g
Carbohydrate	9g
Sugars	9g
Fat	18g
Saturates	5g

cook's tip

Turkey breast steaks would also be very tasty cooked in this way, but should be grilled for 7–8 minutes on each side. Make sure they are thoroughly cooked before serving.

1 Place the pork scallops in a large, shallow, nonmetallic dish. Heat the oil in a small, heavy-bottom pan. Add the bay leaves and stir-fry for 1 minute. Stir in the lemon rind and juice, beer, honey, and juniper berries, and season to taste with salt and pepper.

2 Pour the mixture over the pork, turning to coat. Cover with plastic wrap, let cool, then let marinate in the refrigerator for up to 8 hours.

3 Preheat the barbecue. Drain the pork, reserving the marinade. Core the apple and cut into rings. Cook the pork over medium hot coals, brushing frequently with the reserved marinade, for 5 minutes on each side, or until thoroughly cooked. Cook the apples on the barbecue, brushing frequently with the marinade, for 3 minutes. Transfer the pork to a large serving plate with the apple rings, garnish with parsley sprigs, and serve immediately.

gin & juniper pork

⏱ **cook: 14–18 mins**   ⏳ **prep: 10 mins, plus 8 hrs marinating**   **serves 4**

This dish was originally cooked with wild boar, which is now being farmed and is available in some major supermarkets. It is equally delicious when made with pork chops.

NUTRITIONAL INFORMATION	
Calories	.425
Protein	.32g
Carbohydrate	.10g
Sugars	.8g
Fat	.26g
Saturates	.9g

INGREDIENTS

4 pork chops, about 6 oz/175 g each

¼ cup dry gin

¾ cup orange juice

2 red or white onions, cut in half

6 juniper berries, lightly crushed

thinly pared rind of 1 orange

1 cinnamon stick

1 bay leaf

2 tsp finely chopped fresh thyme

salt and pepper

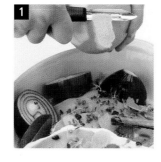

cook's tip

Both red and white onions have a sweeter, milder flavor than yellow onions, which is emphasized by chargrilling. Spanish onions are also mild, but as they are large, use only 1 and cut it into quarters.

1 Place the pork chops in a large, shallow, nonmetallic dish. Pour in the gin and orange juice and add the onion halves. Add the juniper berries, orange rind, cinnamon stick, bay leaf, and thyme and, using a fork, stir well until the pork chops are well coated. Cover with plastic wrap and let marinate in the refrigerator for up to 8 hours.

2 Preheat the barbecue. Drain the pork chops and onions, reserving the marinade. Season the pork chops with salt and pepper and strain the marinade into a small measuring cup.

3 Cook the pork and onions over medium hot coals, brushing frequently with the reserved marinade, for 7–9 minutes on each side, or until thoroughly cooked. Transfer to a large serving plate and serve immediately.

meatballs on sticks

serves 8 **prep: 20 mins** **cook: 10 mins**

These are popular with children and adults alike. Serve with a selection of ready-made or homemade sauces, such as a Tomato Relish (see page 94), heated on the side of the barbecue.

INGREDIENTS

4 pork and herb sausages

½ cup fresh ground beef

1½ cups fresh white bread crumbs

1 onion, finely chopped

2 tbsp chopped mixed fresh herbs, such as parsley, thyme, and sage

1 egg

salt and pepper

corn oil, for brushing

sauces of your choice, to serve

NUTRITIONAL INFORMATION

Calories 132

Protein 9g

Carbohydrate 8g

Sugars 2g

Fat 7g

Saturates 3g

---

variation

Substitute 1 cooked potato and 1 cooked small beet, both finely chopped, for the bread crumbs.

cook's tip

An increasing number of flavored sausages are available, from leek and black pepper to chili, and can be used for these meatballs.

1 Preheat the barbecue. Remove the sausage meat from the skins, place in a large bowl and break up with a fork. Add the ground beef, bread crumbs, onion, herbs, and egg. Season to taste with salt and pepper and stir well with a wooden spoon until thoroughly mixed.

2 Form the mixture into small balls, about the size of a golf ball, between the palms of your hands. Spear each one with a toothpick and brush with oil.

3 Cook over medium hot coals, turning frequently and brushing with more oil as necessary, for 10 minutes, or until cooked through. Transfer to a large serving plate and serve immediately with a choice of sauces.

bacon koftas

serves 4   **prep: 15 mins**   **cook: 10 mins**

Kofta—molded kabobs—are usually made from a spicy mixture of ground lamb. These are economically based on lean bacon. While they are very easy to make, be careful not to overprocess them.

INGREDIENTS

1 small onion

8 oz/225 g lean bacon, rinded and coarsely chopped

1½ cups fresh white bread crumbs

1 tbsp chopped fresh marjoram

grated rind of 1 lemon

1 egg white

pepper

chopped nuts, for coating (optional)

paprika, to dust

snipped fresh chives to garnish

NUTRITIONAL INFORMATION	
Calories	180
Protein	12g
Carbohydrate	12g
Sugars	1g
Fat	10g
Saturates	4g

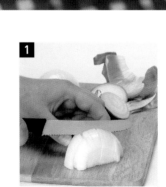

cook's tip

Be careful not to process the kofta mixture for too long. If it becomes too smooth, the koftas will be too sticky to shape, and will lose their delicious texture.

1 Preheat the barbecue, Using a sharp knife, chop the onion, then put it into a food processor with the bacon, bread crumbs, marjoram, lemon rind, and egg white. Season to taste with pepper and process until the mixture is just blended.

2 Divide the bacon mixture into 8 equal portions and form each round a skewer into a fat sausage. Dust the skewered koftas with paprika. If you like, form 4 of the portions into circles rather than sausages, then spread the chopped nuts out on a large, flat plate and roll the circles in them to coat.

3 Cook over hot coals for 10 minutes, turning frequently. Transfer to a large serving plate and serve immediately, garnished with snipped fresh chives.

pigs in blankets

 cook: 15–20 mins   **prep: 15 mins**   **serves 4**

Sausages are traditional fare for the barbecue, but even speciality varieties can a be a little boring. Pigs in blankets, on the other hand, are always fun and delicious.

NUTRITIONAL INFORMATION	
Calories	.499
Protein	.31g
Carbohydrate	.6g
Sugars	.2g
Fat	.39g
Saturates	.16g

INGREDIENTS

4 oz/115 g mozzarella cheese

8 Toulouse sausages

2 tbsp Dijon mustard

8 smoked bacon strips

1 Preheat the barbecue. Thinly slice the mozzarella cheese. Cut a deep slit in the side of each sausage, using a sharp knife. Spread the cut sides with the mustard. Divide the slices of cheese between the sausages and reshape them.

2 Stretch the bacon with a heavy, flat-bladed knife. Wrap 1 bacon strip tightly round each sausage to hold it together. If necessary, secure with a toothpick.

3 Cook over hot coals, turning frequently, for 15–20 minutes. Transfer to a large serving plate and serve immediately.

cook's tip

Toulouse sausages are fairly large cooking sausages made from coarsely chopped pork. They are widely available, but you can substitute other good-quality cooking sausages.

easy mixed grill

cook: 12 mins   **prep: 20 mins**   **serves 4**

NUTRITIONAL INFORMATION

Calories 1083

Protein 42g

Carbohydrate 28g

Sugars 23g

Fat 90g

Saturates 23g

variation

If you like, substitute medallions or noisettes of other meats, such as lamb or chicken, for the steak.

A meat feast, this mixed grill includes everything a red-blooded carnivore could want—sausages, bacon, steak, and kidney. Ideal served with baked potatoes and a crisp green salad.

INGREDIENTS

4 lambs' kidneys	12 bay leaves
6 Canadian bacon strips, rinded	salt and pepper
4 cherry tomatoes	1 quantity Spicy Marinade
4 small fillet steaks or tournedos	(see page 105)
8 small pork sausages	Mustard Butter (see page 112),
4 white mushrooms	to serve

cook's tip

For even cooking, try to ensure that all the pieces of meat are about the same size and make sure that the skewers are not overcrowded, otherwise the meat may not cook properly.

1 Preheat the barbecue. Using a sharp knife, trim the kidneys, cut in half and, using a pair of kitchen scissors, remove the cores. Cut the bacon strips in half across the center, then wrap a piece of bacon round each kidney half and round each cherry tomato.

2 Thread the kidneys, tomatoes, steaks, sausages, mushrooms, and bay leaves alternately onto metal skewers. Season to taste with salt and pepper and brush with the marinade.

3 Cook over medium hot coals, turning and

brushing frequently with the marinade, for 12 minutes. Transfer to a large serving plate and serve immediately with the Mustard Butter.

frankly fabulous skewers

serves 4 **prep: 10 mins** **cook: 40 mins**

A new way with an old favorite—cook frankfurter sausages on the barbecue for a wonderful smoky flavor and an incredibly easy meal. They are served here with garlic toast.

INGREDIENTS

12 frankfurter sausages

2 zucchinis, cut into ½-inch/1-cm slices

2 corn ears, cut into ½-inch/1-cm slices

12 cherry tomatoes

12 pearl onions

2 tbsp olive oil

GARLIC TOAST

2 garlic bulbs

2–3 tbsp olive oil

1 baguette, sliced

salt and pepper

NUTRITIONAL INFORMATION

Calories 620

Protein 19g

Carbohydrate 69g

Sugars 6g

Fat 32g

Saturates 2g

variation

Slice a baguette without cutting it right through. Spread with 2 crushed garlic cloves beaten into 4 oz/115 g butter. Wrap in foil and cook for 15 minutes.

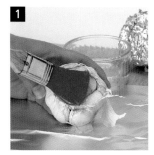

cook's tip

When toasting the baguette, do not put the bread directly over very hot coals. Keep a close watch on them as they only take a few minutes to cook and will burn easily.

1 Preheat the barbecue. To make the garlic toast, slice off the tops of the garlic bulbs. Brush the bulbs with oil and wrap them in foil. Cook over hot coals, turning occasionally, for 30 minutes.

2 Meanwhile, cut each frankfurter sausage into 3 pieces. Thread the frankfurter pieces, zucchini slices, corn slices, cherry tomatoes, and pearl onions alternately onto metal skewers. Brush with olive oil.

3 Cook the skewers over hot coals, turning and brushing frequently with the oil, for 8–10 minutes. Meanwhile, brush the slices of baguette with oil and toast both sides on the barbecue.

Unwrap the garlic bulbs and squeeze the cloves onto the bread. Season to taste with salt and pepper and drizzle over a little extra olive oil, if you like. Transfer the skewers to a large serving plate and serve immediately with the garlic toast.

vegetables

The range of vegetables that can be cooked on the barbecue is immense and some, such as zucchinis, eggplants, red onions, and bell peppers, seem almost designed for the purpose. As they grill, they acquire a delicious sweetness and they look appetisingly attractive.

Some of the recipes in this chapter, for example Greek Vegetable Kabobs (see page 128), Mushroom Burgers (see page 139), and Summer Vegetable Packages (see page 144), can be served as a vegetarian main course, and a number are also suitable for vegans. Other recipes, such as Potato Fans (see page 133), are designed as accompaniments to fish, poultry, meat, or vegetarian dishes. Still others, like Cajun Vegetables (see page 147), can serve either purpose if you adjust the quantities accordingly. Finally, you can serve many of these dishes, such as Stuffed Tomato Packages (see page 132) and Eggplants with Tsatziki (see page 153), as appetizers while you are cooking the main course.

No barbecue would be complete without at least one salad and a selection is even better. A mixed leaf salad is simplicity itself—you can even buy them ready made, complete with a dressing—and you could complement this with one of the four at the end of this chapter. Rice- and pasta-based salads are substantial and popular, and if you are entertaining, impress your guests with the fashionable Lebanese Tabbouleh (see page 156) or the flamboyant Red & Green Salad (see page 159).

greek vegetable kabobs

⏱ **cook: 35 mins**   ⏱ **prep: 20 mins, plus   serves 4**
                          40 mins cooling

NUTRITIONAL INFORMATION

Calories 428

Protein 19g

Carbohydrate 40g

Sugars 21g

Fat 23g

Saturates 4g

variation

Although not authentically Greek, you could serve these kabobs with Aïoli (see page 41). You can substitute feta for the provolone cheese, if you like.

A complete meal on a skewer, these tasty kabobs include a selection of vegetables, cheese, and, perhaps surprisingly, nectarines, in an extremely colorful combination.

INGREDIENTS

2 onions

8 new potatoes, washed
but not peeled

salt

1 eggplant, cut into 8 pieces

8 thick slices cucumber

1 red bell pepper, seeded and cut
into 8 pieces

1 yellow bell pepper, seeded and cut
into 8 pieces

8 oz/225 g provolone cheese,
cut into 8 cubes

2 nectarines, pitted and quartered

8 white mushrooms

2 tbsp olive oil

2 tsp chopped fresh thyme

2 tsp chopped fresh rosemary

1 quantity Tsatziki (see page 153),
to serve

cook's tip

Provolone, an Italian cow's milk cheese, is perfect for barbecues because it softens and chars without melting. Keep a close watch on it as it may burn.

1 Preheat the barbecue. Cut the onions into wedges, then place the onions and potatoes in a pan of lightly salted boiling water and cook for 20 minutes, or until just tender. Drain and let cool. Meanwhile, blanch the eggplant in boiling water for 2 minutes, then add the cucumber and let simmer for 1 minute. Add the bell peppers and let simmer for 2 minutes, then drain and let the vegetables cool.

2 Place the cooled vegetables, cheese, nectarines, and mushrooms in a bowl. Add the olive oil and herbs and toss to coat. Thread the vegetables, cheese, nectarines, and mushrooms onto several metal skewers.

3 Cook the kabobs over hot coals, turning frequently, for 15 minutes. Transfer to a large serving plate and serve immediately with the Tsatziki.

chargrilled vegetables with creamy pesto

serves 4   **prep: 30 mins**   **cook: 8 mins**

Vegetables, especially baby varieties, taste wonderful when cooked on the barbecue. Here they are served with a delicious pesto, which complements them perfectly. Serve with grilled meat.

INGREDIENTS

1 red onion	CREAMY PESTO
1 fennel bulb	4 tbsp fresh basil leaves
4 baby eggplants	1 tbsp pine nuts
4 baby zucchinis	1 garlic clove
1 orange bell pepper	pinch of coarse sea salt
1 red bell pepper	¼ cup freshly grated
2 beefsteak tomatoes	Parmesan cheese
2 tbsp olive oil	¼ cup extra virgin olive oil
salt and pepper	⅔ cup strained plain yogurt
	1 fresh basil sprig, to garnish

NUTRITIONAL INFORMATION

Calories	.313
Protein	.10g
Carbohydrate	.15g
Sugars	.11g
Fat	.24g
Saturates	.6g

variation

If baby vegetables are not available, you can cut 2 eggplants into slices and cut 2 zucchinis in half lengthwise instead.

cook's tip

This homemade pesto mixture, without the added yogurt, will keep in a screw-top jar in the refrigerator for up to 3 days. If it seems to be drying out, pour a layer of olive oil over the top.

1 Preheat the barbecue. To make the creamy pesto, place the basil, pine nuts, garlic, and sea salt in a mortar and pound to a paste with a pestle. Gradually work in the Parmesan cheese, then gradually stir in the oil. Place the yogurt in a small serving bowl and stir in 3–4 tablespoons of the pesto mixture. Cover with plastic wrap and let chill in the refrigerator until required. Store any leftover pesto mixture in a screw-top jar in the refrigerator.

2 Prepare the vegetables. Cut the onion and fennel bulb into wedges, trim the eggplants and zucchinis, seed and halve the bell peppers, and cut the tomatoes in half. Brush the vegetables with oil and season to taste with salt and pepper.

3 Cook the eggplants and bell peppers over hot coals for 3 minutes, then add the zucchinis, onion, and tomatoes and cook, turning occasionally and brushing with more oil if necessary, for an additional 5 minutes. Transfer to a large serving plate and serve with the pesto, garnished with a basil sprig.

stuffed tomato packages

serves 4

prep: 15 mins, plus
15 mins cooling

cook: 20 mins

An unusual filling for stuffed tomatoes, the spinach and cheese are given extra flavor with toasted sunflower seeds.

INGREDIENTS

1 tbsp olive oil

2 tbsp sunflower seeds

1 onion, finely chopped

1 garlic clove, finely chopped

1 lb 2 oz/500 g fresh spinach, thick stalks removed and leaves shredded

pinch of freshly grated nutmeg

salt and pepper

4 beefsteak tomatoes

5 oz/140 g mozzarella cheese, diced

NUTRITIONAL INFORMATION	
Calories 248	
Protein 16g	
Carbohydrate 11g	
Sugars 9g	
Fat 16g	
Saturates 6g	

cook's tip

Dry-roasting sunflower seeds brings out their delicate nutty flavor, but keep stirring constantly as they will burn very easily.

1 Preheat the barbecue. Heat the oil in a heavy-bottom pan. Add the sunflower seeds and cook, stirring constantly, for 2 minutes, or until golden. Add the onion and cook over low heat, stirring occasionally, for 5 minutes, or until softened but not browned. Add the garlic and spinach, cover, and cook for

2–3 minutes, or until the spinach has wilted. Remove the pan from the heat and season to taste with nutmeg, salt and pepper. Let cool.

2 Using a sharp knife, cut off and set aside a thin slice from the top of each tomato and scoop out the flesh with a teaspoon, taking care not to pierce the shell.

Chop the flesh and stir it into the spinach mixture with the mozzarella cheese.

3 Fill the tomato shells with the spinach and cheese mixture and replace the tops. Cut 4 squares of foil, each large enough to enclose a tomato. Place one tomato in the center of each square and fold up the sides to enclose

securely. Cook over hot coals, turning occasionally, for 10 minutes. Serve immediately in the packages.

potato fans

cook: 1 hr   **prep: 5 mins**   **serves 6**

These garlic-flavored roast potatoes make a wonderful alternative to baked potatoes. Allow plenty of time for cooking.

NUTRITIONAL INFORMATION	
Calories	235
Protein	6g
Carbohydrate	46g
Sugars	2g
Fat	4g
Saturates	1g

INGREDIENTS

6 large potatoes, scrubbed but not peeled

2 tbsp garlic-flavored olive oil

1 Preheat the barbecue. Using a sharp knife, make a series of cuts across the potatoes almost all the way through. Cut out 6 squares of foil, each large enough to enclose a potato.

2 Place a potato on each square of foil and brush generously with the garlic-flavored oil. Fold up the sides of the foil to enclose the potatoes completely.

3 Cook over hot coals, turning occasionally, for 1 hour. To serve, open the foil packages and gently pinch the potatoes to open up the fans.

cook's tip

If you do not have any garlic-flavored oil, pour 2 tablespoons olive oil into a bowl, add 1 crushed garlic clove, cover with plastic wrap and let infuse for 2 hours, then use as above.

spicy caribbean kabobs

serves 4   **prep: 20 mins, plus 3 hrs marinating**   **cook: 15 mins**

Bring a taste of the tropics to your barbecue with these sizzling vegetable kabobs. They make a delicious vegetarian main course and are also suitable for vegans.

INGREDIENTS

1 corn ear

1 chayote, peeled and cut into chunks

1 ripe plantain, peeled and cut into thick slices

1 eggplant, cut into chunks

1 red bell pepper, seeded and cut into chunks

1 green bell pepper, seeded and cut into chunks

1 onion, cut into wedges

8 white mushrooms

4 cherry tomatoes

MARINADE

⅔ cup tomato juice

4 tbsp corn oil

4 tbsp lime juice

3 tbsp dark soy sauce

1 shallot, finely chopped

2 garlic cloves, finely chopped

1 fresh green chile, seeded and finely chopped

½ tsp ground cinnamon

pepper

NUTRITIONAL INFORMATION

Calories 250

Protein 5g

Carbohydrate 31g

Sugars 13g

Fat 13g

Saturates 2g

---

variation

If you prefer, replace the green bell pepper with a sweeter orange or red bell pepper and the eggplant with 1 zucchini, cut into chunks.

cook's tip

Chayote, also known as christophene, is a pear-shaped gourd widely used in Caribbean cooking because it readily absorbs spicy flavors. If you cannot find it, use pumpkin or zucchinis instead.

1 Using a sharp knife, remove the husks and silks from the corn and cut into 1-inch/2.5-cm thick slices. Blanch the chayote chunks in boiling water for 2 minutes. Drain, refresh under cold running water, and drain again. Place the chayote chunks in a large bowl with the corn slices and the remaining ingredients.

2 Mix all the marinade ingredients together in a measuring cup, seasoning to taste with pepper. Pour the marinade over the vegetables, tossing to coat. Cover with plastic wrap and let marinate in the refrigerator for 3 hours.

3 Preheat the barbecue. Drain the vegetables, reserving the marinade. Thread the vegetables onto several metal skewers. Cook over hot coals, turning and brushing frequently with the reserved marinade, for 10–15 minutes. Transfer to a large serving plate and serve immediately.

zucchini & cheese packages

cook: 30 mins   **prep: 10 mins**   **serves 4**

NUTRITIONAL INFORMATION

Calories 172

Protein 9g

Carbohydrate 8g

Sugars 6g

Fat 12g

Saturates 1g

variation

If you like, substitute mozzarella cheese or fontina for the feta cheese and replace the mint with the same amount of fresh parsley.

These delicately flavored, melt-in-the-mouth filled zucchinis are ideal if you are serving food to both meat-eaters and vegetarians, as the packages can be cooked in the barbecue embers and so avoid any contact with meat on the grill.

INGREDIENTS

1 small bunch of fresh mint

8 zucchinis

1 tbsp olive oil, plus extra for brushing

4 oz/115 g feta cheese, cut into strips

pepper

cook's tip

Use long-handled tongs to place the packages onto the barbecue embers and to remove them when done. Be careful when opening the packages as they will be extremely hot.

1 Preheat the barbecue. Using a sharp knife, finely chop enough mint to fill 1 tablespoon. Set aside until required. Cut out 8 rectangles of foil, each large enough to enclose a zucchini, and brush lightly with olive oil. Cut a slit along the length of each zucchini and place them on the foil rectangles.

2 Insert strips of feta cheese along the slits in the zucchinis, then drizzle the olive oil over the top, sprinkle with the reserved chopped mint and season to taste with pepper. Fold in the sides of the foil rectangles securely and seal the edges to enclose the cheese-filled zucchinis completely.

3 Bake the packages in the barbecue embers for 30 minutes. Carefully unwrap the packages and serve immediately.

cheese & red onion kabobs

serves 4

**prep: 10 mins, plus
2 hrs marinating**

cook: 10–15 mins

Red onions have a mild, sweet flavor and retain their attractive color when cooked. Here, they are barbecued with apples and salty cheese for a wonderful combination of flavors and textures.

INGREDIENTS

3 red onions

1 lb/450 g provolone cheese, cut into
1-inch/2.5-cm cubes

2 tart eating apples, cored and
cut into wedges

4 tbsp olive oil

1 tbsp cider vinegar

1 tbsp Dijon mustard

1 garlic clove, finely chopped

1 tsp finely chopped sage

salt and pepper

NUTRITIONAL INFORMATION	
Calories	.449
Protein	.21g
Carbohydrate	.16g
Sugars	.13g
Fat	.34g
Saturates	.2g

variation

If you like, you could serve these kabobs with Mild Mustard Sauce (see page 13) or even Sweet-&-Sour Relish (see page 87).

1 Cut the onions into wedges, then place in a large, shallow, nonmetallic dish with the cheese and apples. Mix the oil, vinegar, mustard, garlic, and sage together in a measuring cup and season to taste with salt and pepper.

2 Pour the marinade over the onions, cheese, and apples, tossing to coat. Cover with plastic wrap and let marinate in the refrigerator for 2 hours.

3 Preheat the barbecue. Drain the onions, cheese, and apples, reserving the marinade. Thread the onions, cheese, and apples alternately onto several metal skewers. Cook over hot coals, turning and brushing frequently with the reserved marinade, for 10–15 minutes. Transfer to a large serving plate and serve immediately.

mushroom burgers

cook: 20 mins   **prep: 25 mins, plus 1 hr chilling**   **serves 4**

Like their meaty cousins, homemade veggie burgers taste much more flavorsome—and are usually a good deal healthier— than the storebought varieties.

NUTRITIONAL INFORMATION

Calories	164
Protein	7g
Carbohydrate	24g
Sugars	4g
Fat	5g
Saturates	1g

INGREDIENTS

4 oz/115 g mushrooms

2 tsp corn oil, plus extra for brushing

1 carrot

1 onion

1 zucchini

¼ cup peanuts

2 cups fresh white bread crumbs

1 tbsp chopped fresh parsley

1 tsp yeast extract

salt and pepper

1 tbsp all-purpose flour, for dusting

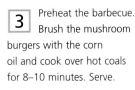

variation

Other nuts could also be used to make the burgers. Try cashew nuts, hazelnuts, or even a mixture of hazelnuts and pistachios.

1 Using a sharp knife, finely chop the mushrooms, then chop the carrot, onion, and zucchini, and set aside. Heat the oil in a heavy-bottom skillet, add the mushrooms and cook, stirring, for 8 minutes, or until all the moisture has evaporated. Using a slotted spoon, transfer the cooked mushrooms to a large bowl.

2 Put the carrot, onion, zucchini, and peanuts into a food processor and process until finely chopped. Transfer to the bowl and stir in the bread crumbs, chopped parsley, and yeast extract. Season to taste with salt and pepper. Lightly flour your hands and form the mixture into 4 patties. Place on a large plate, cover with plastic wrap, and let chill in the refrigerator for at least 1 hour and up to 1 day.

3 Preheat the barbecue. Brush the mushroom burgers with the corn oil and cook over hot coals for 8–10 minutes. Serve.

vegetarian brochettes

cook: 8–10 mins   **prep: 20 mins**   **serves 4**

NUTRITIONAL INFORMATION

Calories 174

Protein 10g

Carbohydrate 11g

Sugars 8g

Fat 10g

Saturates 3g

The great thing about tofu—apart from the fact that it is packed with protein—is its ability to absorb other flavors, in this case a mustard and honey flavored glaze.

INGREDIENTS

2 zucchinis

1 yellow bell pepper, seeded and quartered

8 oz/225 g firm tofu (drained weight)

4 cherry tomatoes

4 pearl onions

8 white mushrooms

HONEY GLAZE

2 tbsp olive oil

1 tbsp Meaux mustard

1 tbsp honey

salt and pepper

variation

You can also make just vegetable brochettes. Omit the tofu and use eggplant chunks, zucchini chunks, and small strips of red bell pepper.

cook's tip

Meaux mustard is made from crushed black mustard seeds and vinegar. It is usually quite hot and is available from most large supermarkets. If you cannot find it, use Dijon mustard instead.

1 Preheat the barbecue. Using a vegetable peeler, peel off strips of skin along the length of the zucchinis to leave alternate yellow and green stripes, then cut each zucchini into 8 thick slices. Cut each of the yellow bell pepper quarters in half. Cut the drained tofu into 1-inch/2.5-cm cubes.

2 Thread the pieces of bell pepper, zucchini slices, tofu cubes, cherry tomatoes, pearl onions, and white mushrooms onto 4 metal skewers. To make the glaze, mix the olive oil, mustard, and honey together in a measuring cup and season to taste with salt and pepper.

3 Brush the brochettes with the honey glaze and cook over medium hot coals, turning and brushing frequently with the glaze, for 8–10 minutes. Serve.

serves 4   **prep: 25 mins, plus 1 hr marinating**   **cook: 30 mins**

This cornucopia of chargrilled vegetables makes a wonderful vegetarian barbecue. Equally, the vegetables can be served as accompaniments to meat or fish.

NUTRITIONAL INFORMATION

Calories 194

Protein 4g

Carbohydrate 13g

Sugars 10g

Fat 15g

Saturates 2g

INGREDIENTS

2 red onions

2 white onions

2 fennel bulbs

6 baby corn

12 cherry tomatoes

4 tbsp olive oil

1 tbsp lemon juice

3 garlic cloves, finely chopped

2 tbsp chopped fresh marjoram

salt and pepper

1 green bell pepper

1 yellow bell pepper

1 orange bell pepper

1 red bell pepper

1 tbsp corn oil

Lemon Mayonnaise (see page 13), to serve

variation

If you prefer, replace the Lemon Mayonnaise with plain Mayonnaise (see page 13) or try Creamy Pesto (see page 130) instead.

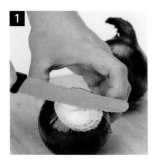

cook's tip

When marinating vegetables, it is not necessary to keep them in the refrigerator. You can leave them in a cool place, covered with plastic wrap.

1 Using a sharp knife, cut the red and white onions in half and set aside until required. Blanch the fennel and baby corn in a large pan of boiling water for 2 minutes. Drain, refresh under cold running water and drain again. Cut the fennel bulbs in half and place in a large, shallow, nonmetallic dish. Cut the baby corn in half across the center and add to the dish with the tomatoes and onions.

2 Mix the oil, lemon juice, garlic, and marjoram in a measuring cup and season to taste with salt and pepper. Pour the mixture over the vegetables, cover, and let marinate for 1 hour.

3 Preheat the barbecue. Drain the vegetables, reserving the marinade. Thread the corn and cherry tomatoes alternately onto presoaked wooden skewers. Brush the bell peppers with oil and cook over medium hot coals, turning, for 10 minutes. Add the onion and fennel to the barbecue and cook, brushing with the marinade, for 5 minutes. Turn the onion and fennel and brush with marinade. Add the skewers, brush with marinade, and cook, turning and brushing frequently with more marinade, for 10 minutes. Transfer the vegetables to a large plate and serve with the Lemon Mayonnaise.

summer vegetable packages

cook: 25–30 mins　　**prep: 15 mins**　　　　serves 4

NUTRITIONAL INFORMATION	
Calories 299	
Protein 3g	
Carbohydrate 17g	
Sugars 6g	
Fat 25g	
Saturates 16g	

variation

If baby vegetables are unavailable, then use larger vegetables cut into small pieces, such as zucchini and carrot sticks and eggplant chunks.

You can use any baby vegetables you like—pattypan squash, corn, and plum tomatoes look attractive and add color. Serve with grilled meat or fish for a substantial barbecue main course.

INGREDIENTS

2 lb 4 oz/1 kg mixed baby vegetables, such as carrots, pattypan squash, corn, plum tomatoes, leeks, zucchinis, and onions

1 lemon

4 oz/115 g unsalted butter

3 tbsp chopped mixed fresh herbs, such as parsley, thyme, and chervil

2 garlic cloves

salt and pepper

cook's tip

It is best to use a double thickness of foil to make packages for cooking on the barbecue so that they don't tear when you turn them.

1 Preheat the barbecue. Cut out 4 x 12-inch/ 30-cm squares of foil and divide the vegetables equally between them.

2 Using a grater, finely grate the lemon rind, then squeeze the juice from the lemon and set aside until required. Put the lemon rind, butter, herbs, and garlic into a food processor and process until blended, then season to taste with salt and pepper. Alternatively, beat together in a bowl until blended.

3 Divide the butter equally between the vegetables, dotting it on top. Fold up the sides of the foil to enclose the vegetables, sealing securely. Cook over medium hot coals, turning occasionally, for 25–30 minutes. Open the packages, sprinkle with the reserved lemon juice, and serve immediately.

corn with blue cheese dressing

serves 6   **prep: 15 mins** ⏲   **cook: 15–20 mins** ⏲

Corn is delicious grilled on the barbecue. Cook them as soon after purchase as possible because they quickly lose their sweetness as their natural sugars convert to starch.

INGREDIENTS

5 oz/140 g Danablu cheese

5 oz/140 g curd cheese

½ cup strained plain yogurt

salt and pepper

6 corn ears in their husks

NUTRITIONAL INFORMATION

Calories 255

Protein 12g

Carbohydrate 21g

Sugars 4g

Fat 14g

Saturates 8g

cook's tip

When buying corn, always make sure that they are as fresh as possible and only choose ones that have golden tassels and are heavy.

1 Preheat the barbecue. Crumble the Danablu cheese, then place in a bowl. Beat with a wooden spoon until creamy. Beat in the curd cheese until thoroughly blended. Gradually beat in the yogurt and season to taste with salt and pepper. Cover with plastic wrap and let chill in the refrigerator until required.

2 Fold back the husks on each corn and remove the silks. Smooth the husks back into place. Cut out 6 rectangles of foil, each large enough to enclose a corn. Wrap the corn in the foil.

3 Cook the corn over hot coals, turning frequently, for 15–20 minutes. Unwrap the corn and discard the foil. Peel back the husk on one side of each and trim off with a sharp knife or kitchen scissors. Serve immediately with the blue cheese dressing.

cajun vegetables

cook: 12–15 mins   **prep: 10 mins**   **serves 4**

These spicy vegetables would be a perfect accompaniment to Blackened Chicken (see page 71) and would also go well with Caribbean Sea Bass (see page 20).

NUTRITIONAL INFORMATION

Calories 244

Protein 5g

Carbohydrate 41g

Sugars 8g

Fat 8g

Saturates 4g

INGREDIENTS

4 corn ears

2 sweet potatoes

1 oz/25 g butter, melted

SPICE MIX

2 teaspoons paprika

1 teaspoon ground cumin

1 teaspoon ground coriander

1 teaspoon ground black pepper

½–1 teaspoon chili powder

1 Preheat the barbecue. To make the spice mix, mix all the ingredients together in a small bowl.

2 Remove the husks and silks from the corn, then cut each corn into 4 equal chunks. Cut the sweet potatoes into thick slices, but do not peel. Brush the corn chunks and sweet potato slices with melted butter and sprinkle with some spice mix.

3 Cook the corn and sweet potatoes over medium hot coals, turning frequently, for 12–15 minutes. Brush with more melted butter and sprinkle with extra spice mixture during cooking.

Transfer the corn and sweet potatoes to a large serving plate and serve immediately.

cook's tip

The flesh of sweet potatoes varies in color from white to orange. Not only are the orange-fleshed varieties more attractive, they also contain more nutrients.

eggplant & sweet potato rolls

serves 4–6   **prep: 30 mins** ⟲   **cook: 45–50 mins** ⟲

*Partially cooked in advance, these attractive little rolls with
a tasty filling are baked in foil packages.*

INGREDIENTS

1 lb/450 g sweet potatoes	1½ tsp paprika
salt and black pepper	1½ tsp curry powder
4 scallions, chopped	1½ tsp celery salt
6 oz/175 g Gruyère cheese, diced	1 tsp superfine sugar
1 red bell pepper, seeded and chopped	1 tbsp garlic granules
1 garlic clove, crushed	4 large eggplants
1 tsp chopped fresh thyme	3 tbsp olive oil, plus extra
scant ¼ cup all-purpose flour	for brushing

NUTRITIONAL INFORMATION

Calories	.452
Protein	.17g
Carbohydrate	.39g
Sugars	.16g
Fat	.27g
Saturates	.11g

variation

Emmental cheese would also work
well in this dish. If you like, substitute
the same quantity of Emmental cheese
for the Gruyère cheese.

cook's tip

Salting eggplant slices will
prevent them from soaking up
too much oil during cooking.
Place in a strainer, sprinkle
with salt, and let stand for
30 minutes. Rinse and pat dry.

1 Preheat the barbecue.
Cook the sweet
potatoes in a pan of boiling
salted water for 20 minutes, or
until tender. Drain and let
stand until cool enough to
handle. Peel and mash in a
large bowl until smooth. Add
the scallions, cheese, red bell
pepper, garlic, and thyme,
and season to taste with salt
and pepper.

2 Place the flour on a
large plate and stir in
the paprika, curry powder,
celery salt, sugar, and garlic
granules. Slice each eggplant
lengthwise into quarters and
dust with the seasoned flour.
Heat half the olive oil in a
large, heavy-bottom skillet.
Add the eggplant slices, in
batches, and cook until just
golden brown, adding more oil

as necessary. Remove with
a slotted spoon and let cool.

3 Place a spoonful of the
sweet potato mixture
on each eggplant slice and roll
up. Cut out 4 x 12-inch/30-cm
squares of foil and brush with
oil. Place 4 eggplant rolls on
each square and fold up the
sides to enclose the rolls. Cook
over medium hot coals,

turning occasionally, for
25–30 minutes. Unwrap the
packages and transfer the rolls
to a large serving dish.
Serve immediately.

indian kabobs

cook: 10–12 mins   **prep: 15 mins**   **serves 4**

NUTRITIONAL INFORMATION

Calories	.160
Protein	.7g
Carbohydrate	.22g
Sugars	.22g
Fat	.6g
Saturates	.1g

variation

Replace the cauliflower florets with broccoli florets and the orange bell pepper with red or green bell pepper.

Vegetables, fruit, and cheese, brushed with a spicy glaze, need no more than a plate of salad to make a delicious vegetarian meal.

INGREDIENTS

6 oz/175 g panir	**GLAZE**
8 cherry tomatoes	2 tbsp lime juice
1 orange bell pepper, seeded and cut	2 tbsp chili sauce
into pieces	1 tbsp vegetable oil
8 cauliflower florets	1 tbsp honey
3 pineapple slices, cut into quarters	1 tbsp water
1 mango, peeled, seeded, and	pinch of ground cumin
cut into cubes	salt and pepper

cook's tip

Panir is a soft Indian cheese made by curdling milk with lemon juice, before straining and pressing flat. It is available from Asian markets, but tofu could be used as a substitute.

1 Preheat the barbecue. Place all the ingredients for the glaze in a small bowl, seasoning to taste with salt and pepper. Using a balloon whisk, whisk until thoroughly blended. Set aside until required.

2 Using a sharp knife, cut the panir into 1-inch/2.5-cm cubes. Thread the tomatoes, orange bell pepper pieces, cauliflower florets, pineapple pieces, mango cubes, and panir cubes onto 4 long metal skewers.

3 Brush the kabobs with the glaze and cook over medium hot coals, turning and brushing frequently with the glaze, for 10–12 minutes. Serve the kabobs immediately.

prune, apricot & onion skewers

serves 4 | **prep: 15 mins** | **cook: 25 mins**

These flavorsome, fruity skewers would go well with plainly grilled pork chops, duck breasts, lamb steaks, or kabobs, as they will counteract the richness of the meat.

INGREDIENTS

1 lb 2 oz/500 g pearl onions

¾ cup prunes, pitted

1⅓ cups dried apricots, pitted

2-inch/5-cm cinnamon stick

1 cup white wine

2 tbsp chili sauce

2 tbsp corn oil

NUTRITIONAL INFORMATION

Calories 292

Protein 5g

Carbohydrate 48g

Sugars 45g

Fat 6g

Saturates 1g

cook's tip

Pearl onions are also known as baby onions and have a delicate sweet flavor. If you cannot find them, then use shallots or 1 white onion, cut into chunks.

1 Cut the tops off the onions and peel off the skin. Set aside until required. Place the prunes, apricots, cinnamon, and wine in a heavy-bottom pan and bring to a boil. Reduce the heat and let simmer for 5 minutes. Drain, reserving the cooking liquid, and leave the fruit until cool enough to handle.

2 Return the cooking liquid and cinnamon stick to the pan, bring back to a boil and boil until reduced by half. Remove the pan from the heat and remove and discard the cinnamon stick. Stir in the chili sauce and oil.

3 Thread the prunes, apricots, and onions onto several metal skewers.

Cook over medium hot coals, turning and brushing frequently with the wine mixture, for 10 minutes. Serve immediately.

eggplants with tsatziki

cook: 10 mins   **prep: 15 minutes**   **serves 4**

This makes a tasty appetizer for a barbecue party or can be served as part of a vegetarian meze with Stuffed Tomato Packages (see page 132),or Zucchini & Cheese Packages (see page 136).

NUTRITIONAL INFORMATION

Calories 137

Protein 5g

Carbohydrate 5g

Sugars 5g

Fat 11g

Saturates 4g

INGREDIENTS

2 tbsp olive oil

salt and pepper

2 eggplants, thinly sliced

TSATZIKI

½ cucumber

generous ¾ cup strained plain yogurt

4 scallions, finely chopped

1 garlic clove, finely chopped

3 tbsp chopped fresh mint

salt and pepper

1 fresh mint sprig, to garnish

cook's tip

An alternative dip to serve with the eggplants can be made by blending 1¼ cups sour cream with 2 crushed garlic cloves. Season and let chill before serving.

1 Preheat the barbecue. To make the tsatziki, finely chop the cucumber. Place the yogurt in a bowl and beat well until smooth. Stir in the cucumber, scallions, garlic, and mint. Season to taste with salt and pepper. Transfer to a serving bowl, cover with plastic wrap and let chill in the refrigerator until required.

2 Season the olive oil with salt and pepper, then brush the eggplant slices with the oil.

3 Cook the eggplants over hot coals for 5 minutes on each side, brushing with more oil, if necessary. Transfer to a large serving plate and serve immediately with the tsatziki, garnished with a mint sprig.

tropical rice salad

serves 4   **prep: 20 mins**   **cook: 15 mins**

Rice salads are always popular and this colorful, fruity mixture goes especially well with barbecued meat or chicken.

INGREDIENTS

½ cup long-grain rice

salt and pepper

4 scallions

8 oz/225 g canned pineapple pieces in natural juice

7 oz/200 g canned corn, drained

2 red bell peppers, seeded and diced

3 tbsp golden raisins

DRESSING

1 tbsp peanut oil

1 tbsp hazelnut oil

1 tbsp light soy sauce

1 garlic clove, finely chopped

1 tsp chopped fresh gingerroot

NUTRITIONAL INFORMATION

Calories 300

Protein 5g

Carbohydrate 57g

Sugars 26g

Fat 7g

Saturates 1g

---

variation

Try other flavored nut oils, such as walnut oil or sesame oil. You can also substitute corn oil for the peanut oil, if you like.

---

cook's tip

Before using long-grain rice, rinse it thoroughly under cold running water to remove any impurities. Once cooked, it is important to rinse it again to remove all the excess starch.

1 Cook the rice in a large pan of lightly salted boiling water for 15 minutes, or until tender. Drain thoroughly and rinse under cold running water. Place the rice in a large serving bowl.

2 Using a sharp knife, finely chop the scallions. Drain the pineapple pieces, reserving the juice in a measuring cup. Add the pineapple pieces, corn, red bell peppers, chopped scallions, and golden raisins to the rice and mix lightly.

3 Add all the dressing ingredients to the reserved pineapple juice, whisking well, and season to taste with salt and pepper. Pour the dressing over the salad and toss until the salad is thoroughly coated. Serve immediately.

serves 4   **prep: 10 mins, plus 1 hr** ⏱
30 mins standing/marinating   **cook: 0 mins** ♨

This Middle Eastern salad is increasingly fashionable. It is a classic accompaniment for lamb, but goes well with most grilled meat.

INGREDIENTS

1 cup bulgur wheat

3 tbsp extra virgin olive oil

4 tbsp lemon juice

salt and pepper

4 scallions

1 green bell pepper, seeded and sliced

4 tomatoes, chopped

2 tbsp chopped fresh parsley

2 tbsp chopped fresh mint

8 black olives, pitted

fresh mint sprigs, to garnish

NUTRITIONAL INFORMATION

Calories 265

Protein 6g

Carbohydrate 37g

Sugars 4g

Fat 11g

Saturates 2g

variation

Use different types of fresh tomatoes—try vine-ripened tomatoes, which have a delicate, sweet flavor, or cherry tomatoes, cut in half.

  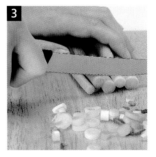

cook's tip

The grains of bulgur wheat have been cracked by boiling and so are partially cooked, so all it needs is rehydrating. Don't make this salad too far in advance as it may go soggy.

1 Place the bulgur wheat in a large bowl and add enough cold water to cover. Let stand for 30 minutes, or until the wheat has doubled in size. Drain well and press out as much liquid as possible. Spread out the wheat on paper towels to dry.

2 Place the wheat in a serving bowl. Mix the olive oil and lemon juice together in a measuring cup and season to taste with salt and pepper. Pour the lemon mixture over the wheat and let marinate for 1 hour.

3 Using a sharp knife, finely chop the scallions, then add to the salad with the green bell pepper, tomatoes, parsley, and mint, and toss lightly to mix. Top the salad with the olives and garnish with fresh mint sprigs, then serve.

cheese & walnut pasta salad

serves 4   **prep: 15 mins** ⏲   **cook: 10–15 mins** ⏲

This is an ideal salad to serve with a barbecue, as it is not just a pasta salad, which can seem a little mundane, but also includes a colorful mix of crisp salad greens.

INGREDIENTS

8 oz/225 g dried fusilli

salt and pepper

8 oz/225 g Gorgonzola cheese

3½ oz/100 g mixed salad greens, such
as oak leaf lettuce, baby spinach,
arugula, and corn salad

1 cup walnut halves

4 tbsp corn oil

2 tbsp walnut oil

2 tbsp red wine vinegar

NUTRITIONAL INFORMATION	
Calories	.759
Protein	.17g
Carbohydrate	.43g
Sugars	.3g
Fat	.56g
Saturates	.17g

cook's tip

You can substitute another piquant cheese for the Gorgonzola, such as Stilton, goat cheese, or even feta, if you prefer.

1 Cook the pasta in a large pan of lightly salted boiling water for 8–10 minutes, or until tender, but still firm to the bite. Drain, rinse under cold running water and drain again.

2 Using a sharp knife, cut the Gorgonzola cheese into cubes. Place the salad leaves in a large serving bowl and add the cooked pasta. Sprinkle the Gorgonzola cheese on top.

3 Preheat the broiler to medium. Place the walnut halves on a large baking sheet and cook under the broiler for a few minutes, or until lightly toasted. Let cool. Mix the corn oil, walnut oil, and wine vinegar together in a measuring cup and season to taste with salt and pepper. Pour the dressing over the salad, toss lightly, then top with the toasted walnuts.

red & green salad

cook: 5 mins prep: 10 mins serves 4

Beet and orange is a classic combination and here they are combined with tender, baby spinach leaves to make a dramatic and colorful warm salad.

NUTRITIONAL INFORMATION	
Calories	173
Protein	5g
Carbohydrate	20g
Sugars	18g
Fat	9g
Saturates	1g

INGREDIENTS

1 lb 7 oz/650 g cooked beet

3 tbsp extra virgin olive oil

juice of 1 orange

1 tsp superfine sugar

1 tsp fennel seeds

salt and pepper

4 oz/115 g fresh baby spinach leaves

cook's tip

To cook beet, trim the leaves and rinse. Cook in a pan of salted water for 1 hour, or until tender. Drain and let cool. Rub off the skin and trim the root.

1 Using a sharp knife, dice the cooked beet and set aside until required. Heat the olive oil in a small, heavy-bottom pan. Add the orange juice, sugar and fennel seeds and season to taste with salt and pepper. Stir constantly until the sugar has dissolved.

2 Add the reserved beet to the pan and stir gently to coat. Remove the pan from the heat.

3 Arrange the baby spinach leaves in a large salad bowl. Spoon the warmed beet on top and serve immediately.

desserts

*Cooking desserts on the barbecue is not very common, perhaps because everyone
is already full of grilled food, the cook is fed up with wielding the tongs, or the barbecue
grill is smothered with soy sauce or whole-grain mustard. This is rather a pity because
many fruits acquire a new character when chargrilled.*

*A second barbecue will avoid the residues of savory dishes. Most desserts cook
quite quickly, so an inexpensive disposable barbecue would be perfectly satisfactory for
recipes such as Totally Tropical Pineapple (see page 162) or Cinnamon Fruit with Chocolate
Smoothie (see page 170). Alternatively, choose one of the recipes, such as Coconut Apples
(see page 166), where the fruit is wrapped in foil before cooking.*

*If you are hot and bothered and never want to see a briquette again, try persuading another
member of the family to take over cooking the dessert. Many desserts benefit from prolonged
marinating, so you can prepare them in advance and let someone else turn and brush them.*

*Finally, have you considered serving a barbecued dessert at the end of a different kind of meal?
For example, if you are entertaining guests to an al fresco lunch of cold dishes that you have
made in advance, the barbecue can be heating up while you are eating the main course and you
can then cook the dessert. This would make a delightful and unusual finale to the meal.*

totally tropical pineapple

cook: 6–8 mins **prep: 15 mins** **serves 4**

NUTRITIONAL INFORMATION	
Calories	206
Protein	1g
Carbohydrate	20g
Sugars	20g
Fat	12g
Saturates	7g

The delicious aroma of fresh pineapple and rum as this succulent, mouthwatering dessert is cooking will transport you to a Caribbean beach. The ground ginger adds just a touch of spice.

INGREDIENTS

1 pineapple

3 tbsp dark rum

2 tbsp brown sugar

1 tsp ground ginger

4 tbsp unsalted butter, melted

variation

If you prefer, you can cut the pineapple into cubes or quarters and thread on skewers before brushing with the rum mixture and cooking.

cook's tip

If possible, use a separate grill rack or even barbecue to cook the pineapple on. It is best to use a pair of long-handled tongs to turn the pineapple rings over while cooking.

1 Preheat the barbecue. Using a sharp knife, cut off the crown of the pineapple, then cut the fruit into ¾-inch/2-cm thick slices. Cut away the peel from each slice and flick out the "eyes" with the tip of the knife. Stamp out the cores with an apple corer or small cookie cutter.

2 Mix the rum, sugar, ginger, and butter together in a measuring cup, stirring constantly, until the sugar has dissolved. Brush the pineapple rings with the rum mixture.

3 Cook the pineapple rings over hot coals for 3–4 minutes on each side.

Transfer to serving plates and serve immediately with the remaining rum mixture poured over them.

caramelized fruit

serves 4   **prep: 15 mins, plus 1 hr marinating**   **cook: 5 mins**

It is quite unusual to include fresh strawberries in a chargrilled fruit salad, but they work surprising well and taste delicious.

INGREDIENTS

⅔ cup medium sherry

½ cup superfine sugar

4 peaches

1 ogen melon, halved and seeded

generous 1 cup strawberries

NUTRITIONAL INFORMATION	
Calories	.234
Protein	.2g
Carbohydrate	.49g
Sugars	.49g
Fat	.0g
Saturates	.0g

cook's tip

Choose large, ripe strawberries for this dish. Do not hull them and make sure that they are turned frequently during cooking to prevent burning.

1 Mix the sherry and sugar together in a large bowl, stirring constantly, until the sugar has dissolved.

2 Cut the peaches in half and remove the pits, then place in a bowl and cover with boiling water. Let stand for 15–20 seconds, then remove with a slotted spoon. Peel off the skin. Cut the melon halves into wedges and cut the flesh away from the skin. Add the melon wedges, peach halves, and strawberries to the sherry mixture, tossing gently to coat. Cover with plastic wrap and let marinate in the refrigerator for 1 hour.

3 Preheat the barbecue. Drain the fruit, reserving the marinade. Cook the melon and peaches over hot coals for 3 minutes, then add the strawberries and cook for an additional 2 minutes. Turn the fruit and brush frequently with the reserved marinade. Serve.

special peach melba

⏱ **cook: 3–5 mins**   ⏱ **prep: 15 mins, plus 1 hr marinating**   **serves 4**

The elegant simplicity of this rich, fruity dessert makes it the perfect end to a special occasion barbecue party.

NUTRITIONAL INFORMATION	
Calories	.480
Protein	.8g
Carbohydrate	.83g
Sugars	.79g
Fat	.15g
Saturates	.10g

INGREDIENTS

2 large peaches, peeled, halved, and pitted

1 tbsp light brown sugar

1 tbsp amaretto liqueur

2 cups fresh raspberries, plus extra to decorate

1 cup confectioners' sugar

1 pint/600 ml vanilla ice cream

cook's tip

For the best results, remove the vanilla ice cream from the freezer 20 minutes before serving and leave in the refrigerator. This allows it to soften slightly and makes it easier to scoop.

1 Place the peach halves in a large, shallow dish and sprinkle with the brown sugar. Pour the amaretto liqueur over them, cover with plastic wrap and let marinate for 1 hour.

2 Meanwhile, using the back of a spoon, press the raspberries through a fine strainer set over a bowl.

Discard the contents of the strainer. Stir the confectioners' sugar into the raspberry purée. Cover the bowl with plastic wrap and let chill in the refrigerator until required.

3 Preheat the barbecue. Drain the peach halves, reserving the marinade. Cook over hot coals, turning and brushing frequently with the

reserved marinade, for 3–5 minutes. To serve, put 2 scoops of vanilla ice cream in each of 4 sundae glasses, top with a peach half, and spoon the raspberry sauce over it. Decorate with whole raspberries and serve.

coconut apples

serves 4 **prep: 10 mins** **cook: 15–20 mins**

This is a barbecue variation of the ever-popular dessert of baked apples, but instead of being filled with dried fruit, they are layered with a rich combination of jelly and coconut.

INGREDIENTS

2 tsp unsalted butter

4 tbsp ginger and apple jelly

scant 1 cup desiccated coconut

pinch of ground cinnamon

4 cooking apples

heavy cream or ice cream, to serve
(optional)

NUTRITIONAL INFORMATION

Calories 312

Protein 2g

Carbohydrate 32g

Sugars 32g

Fat 20g

Saturates 17g

variation

You can substitute large, firm pears for the apples and use different flavored jellys, such as apricot.

cook's tip

Desiccated coconut is usually available from most large supermarkets and specialist foodstores. Store in an airtight container and use it quickly.

1 Preheat the barbecue. Cut out 4 squares of foil, each large enough to enclose 1 apple, and lightly grease with the unsalted butter. Mix the ginger and apple jelly and coconut together in a small bowl and stir in cinnamon to taste.

2 Core the apples, but don't peel them. Cut each apple horizontally into 3 slices. Spread the mixture between the apple slices and reassemble the apples. Place an apple on each sheet of foil and fold up the sides to enclose securely.

3 Cook the apples over hot coals for 15–20 minutes. Serve immediately with cream or ice cream, if you like.

mixed fruit kabobs

serves 4 **prep: 20 mins, plus 1 hr marinating** **cook: 5–7 mins**

You can use almost any firm-fleshed fruit to make these colorful, quick and easy kabobs. Remember to soak the wooden skewers in cold water before using to prevent burning.

INGREDIENTS

2 nectarines, halved and pitted

2 kiwifruit

4 red plums

1 mango, peeled, halved, and seeded

2 bananas, peeled and thickly sliced

8 strawberries, hulled

1 tbsp honey

3 tbsp Cointreau

NUTRITIONAL INFORMATION

Calories 185

Protein 3g

Carbohydrate 38g

Sugars 37g

Fat 1g

Saturates 0g

cook's tip

If serving these kabobs to children, omit the Cointreau and use orange juice instead. It may be easier to remove the cooked fruit from the skewers before serving.

1 Cut the nectarine halves in half again and place in a large, shallow dish. Peel and quarter the kiwifruit. Cut the plums in half and remove the pits. Cut the mango flesh into chunks and add to the dish with the kiwifruit, plums, bananas, and strawberries.

2 Mix the honey and Cointreau together in a measuring cup until blended. Pour the mixture over the fruit and toss to coat. Cover with plastic wrap and let marinate in the refrigerator for 1 hour.

3 Preheat the barbecue. Drain the fruit, reserving the marinade. Thread the fruit onto several presoaked wooden skewers and cook over medium hot coals, turning and brushing frequently with the reserved marinade, for 5–7 minutes, then serve.

fruit packages

⏱ **cook: 4 mins**   ⏱ **prep: 15 mins**   **serves 4**

If you don't have a "spare" barbecue, cooking fruit in a package is a good idea for dessert, as it avoids any contamination from earlier savory courses and keeps the fruit wonderfully succulent.

NUTRITIONAL INFORMATION	
Calories	112
Protein	2g
Carbohydrate	28g
Sugars	28g
Fat	0g
Saturates	0g

INGREDIENTS

2 oranges

2 eating apples

juice of 1 lemon

2 pears

4 tsp brown sugar

cook's tip

Brushing a little lemon juice onto cut fruit, such as apples and pears, prevents them from discoloring. It also enhances their flavor

1 Preheat the barbecue. Peel the oranges, carefully removing all the pith. Cut each orange horizontally into 6 slices. Core the apples, but do not peel. Cut each apple horizontally into 6 slices. Brush the slices with lemon juice. Peel and core the pears, then cut each of them horizontally into 6 slices. Brush the slices with lemon juice.

2 Cut out 4 large squares of foil. Divide the fruit slices equally between the squares and sprinkle each pile with 1 teaspoon of the sugar. Fold up the sides of the squares to enclose the fruit securely.

3 Cook the packages over medium hot coals for about 4 minutes. Serve immediately in the packages.

serves 4   **prep: 10 mins** ⌚   **cook: 10 mins** ⏲

Fresh fruit kabobs are coated with spicy butter before grilling and are then served with an easy-to-prepare, rich chocolate sauce.

INGREDIENTS

4 slices fresh pineapple

2 kiwifruit, peeled and quartered

12 strawberries, hulled

1 tbsp melted unsalted butter

1 tsp ground cinnamon

1 tbsp orange juice

SMOOTHIE

8 oz/225 g semisweet chocolate

1 oz/25 g unsalted butter

⅔ cup superfine sugar

½ cup evaporated milk

1 tsp vanilla extract

4 tbsp Kahlúa

NUTRITIONAL INFORMATION	
Calories	.643
Protein	.6g
Carbohydrate	.91g
Sugars	.88g
Fat	.29g
Saturates	.17g

cook's tip

Always try to find the best-quality chocolate that you can buy. Try to break the chocolate into pieces roughly the same size, so they will all melt at the same rate.

1 Preheat the barbecue. To make the smoothie, break the chocolate into pieces and melt with the butter in a pan over low heat. Stir in the sugar and evaporated milk and cook, stirring, until the sugar has dissolved and the sauce has thickened. Transfer to a heatproof bowl and set on the side of the barbecue to keep hot.

2 Cut the pineapple slices into chunks. Thread the pineapple chunks, kiwifruit, and strawberries alternately onto several presoaked wooden skewers. Mix the butter, cinnamon and orange juice together in a small bowl. Brush the fruit kabobs all over with the cinnamon butter.

3 Cook the kabobs over hot coals, turning and brushing frequently with any remaining cinnamon butter, for 3–5 minutes, or until golden. Just before serving, stir the vanilla extract and Kahlúa into the smoothie.

stuffed pears

cook: 20 mins **prep: 20 mins** **serves 4**

It is a popular practice to sprinkle strawberries with pepper to bring out their flavor—this is equally effective with other fruit.

NUTRITIONAL INFORMATION	
Calories	184
Protein	1g
Carbohydrate	42g
Sugars	42g
Fat	3g
Saturates	2g

INGREDIENTS

2 tsp unsalted butter, for greasing

4 firm dessert pears

2 tbsp lemon juice

4 tbsp rosehip syrup

1 tsp green peppercorns, lightly crushed

1 cup red currants

4 tbsp superfine sugar

ice cream, to serve

cook's tip

When buying pears, always choose slightly underripe ones and let them ripen at room temperature. Choose varieties such as Anjou and Bartlett.

1 Preheat the barbecue. Cut out 4 squares of foil, each large enough to enclose the pears, and grease with the butter. Halve and core the pears, but do not peel. Brush the cut surfaces with lemon juice. Place 2 pear halves on each of the foil squares, brush them with the rosehip syrup and sprinkle with the peppercorns.

2 Place the red currants in a bowl and sprinkle with the sugar. Spoon the red currant mixture into the cavities of the pears. Fold up the sides of the foil to enclose the pears securely.

3 Cook over hot coals for 20 minutes. Serve immediately with ice cream.

barbecued fruit with maple syrup

serves 4   **prep: 20 mins** ⏲   **cook: 10 mins** 🍳

Slices of juicy fruit are coated in a rich maple syrup sauce as they cook in little packages on the barbecue.

INGREDIENTS

1 papaya

1 mango, peeled and seeded

2 bananas

2 peaches, halved, pitted, and peeled

1 ogen melon, halved and seeded

4 oz/115 g unsalted butter, diced

4 tbsp maple syrup

pinch of ground allspice

NUTRITIONAL INFORMATION

Calories	.383
Protein	.2g
Carbohydrate	.42g
Sugars	.40g
Fat	.24g
Saturates	.16g

cook's tip

Look for "pure" or "100 percent" maple syrup, which is expensive. Cheaper varieties may be blended with other types of syrup.

1 Preheat the barbecue. Cut out 4 large squares of foil. Using a sharp knife, cut the papaya in half and remove the seeds, then cut the halves into thick slices and peel off the skin. Thickly slice the mango and remove the seed, then peel off the skin and cut the flesh into slices. Peel the bananas and cut in half lengthwise. Slice the peach halves. Cut the melon halves into thin wedges, then cut the flesh away from the rind. Divide the fruit between the foil squares.

2 Put the butter and maple syrup into a food processor and process until thoroughly blended and smooth. Divide the flavored butter between the packages of fruit and sprinkle with a little allspice. Fold up the sides of the foil to enclose the fruit securely.

3 Cook over medium hot coals, turning occasionally, for 10 minutes. Remove from the packages and serve immediately.

banana sizzles

cook: 6–8 mins **prep: 10 mins** **serves 4**

Bananas are particularly sweet and delicious when grilled—and conveniently come with their own protective wrapping.

NUTRITIONAL INFORMATION	
Calories	.284
Protein	.2g
Carbohydrate	.41g
Sugars	.38g
Fat	.12g
Saturates	.8g

INGREDIENTS

3 tbsp butter, softened

2 tbsp dark rum

1 tbsp orange juice

4 tbsp brown sugar

pinch of ground cinnamon

4 bananas

orange zest, to decorate

1 Preheat the barbecue. Beat the butter with the rum, orange juice, sugar, and cinnamon in a small bowl until thoroughly blended and smooth.

2 Place the bananas, without peeling, over hot coals and cook, turning frequently, for 6–8 minutes, or until the skins are blackened.

3 Transfer the bananas to serving plates, slit the skins and cut partially through the flesh lengthwise. Divide the flavored butter between the bananas, decorate with orange zest, and serve.

cook's tip

Try cooking the bananas in foil. Cut them in half lengthwise without peeling. Spread the butter over the cut surfaces and reassemble. Wrap in foil. Cook over medium hot coals for 5–10 minutes.

index